AF328470

UPSTART

Alexandria Procter

Co-founder of DigsConnect,
SA's startup sensation

mf

Melinda Ferguson Books,
an imprint of NB Publishers, a division of Media24 Boeke (Pty) Ltd
40 Heerengracht, Cape Town, South Africa
PO Box 879, Cape Town 8000, South Africa
www.nb.co.za

Cover design and typography: Wilna Combrinck
Editor: Melinda Ferguson
Proofreader: Riaan Wolmarans
Set in Sabon LT Pro
Printed and bound by CTP Printers, Cape Town

First published by Melinda Ferguson Books 2024
First edition, first impression

ISBN: 978-1-990973-58-1 (Print)
ISBN: 978-1-990973-59-8 (ePub)

This book is dedicated to everyone who's fighting for something. Everyone at the bottom, looking up, fighting their way through the red tape, against despotic governments and through suffering. It's for those souls who are fighting for a dream, fighting for a better future, fighting to create, fighting through depression, through heartbreak, through exhaustion, against incompetence and oppression. This book is for you.

I've come to believe that nothing worth having comes easily. It's the struggle for it that gives it value. It's the blood that it drains from you that gives it life. That's what we are born for: the struggle for freedom, for love, for a better future, for our wildness and authenticity, for a shot at greatness.

Your life is your own. Write your story. Live it. Because this is it – this is your shot. This is your chance to run. So, stretch your legs and give it your all.

In the greater sense, you have nothing to lose. Do something spectacular, shine – shine, goddammit! Make us laugh, make us cry, make us proud. Leave your mark with all the love you hold, all your potential made manifest.

Bad times are inevitable, but how you face them will become Your Story. Fight well.

"Caelum certe patet, ibimus illi."
("Surely the sky lies open: let us go that way!")
– Ovid, *Metamorphoses*

CONTENTS

Introduction   13

Chapter 1
Love Shack   19

Chapter 2
Add another zero   23

Chapter 3
Dropping cash   27

Chapter 4
Instant chemistry   36

Chapter 5
From dropout to flying high   42

Chapter 6
Born (nearly) free   47

Chapter 7
Practical Pete & The Great Heid   55

Chapter 8
An education   60

Chapter 9
From india with love   69

Chapter 10
A night in prison   76

Chapter 11
My inglorious failure   82

Chapter 12
Licking my wounds on Kilimanjaro   87
Chapter 13
Do or die   91
Chapter 14
#FeesMustFall & the student housing crisis   98
Chapter 15
Black hole   105
Chapter 16
Meeting Greg   115
Chapter 17
Creating DigsConnect in my childhood bedroom   122
Chapter 18
Dropout   134
Chapter 19
Don't drink the Kool-Aid   143
Chapter 20
President Proc   148
Chapter 21
A global crisis   157
Chapter 22
Locked down   161
Chapter 23
Poached   169
Chapter 24
Perspective   174
Chapter 25
Sick ... And tired   180
Chapter 26
You can't eat the Freedom Charter   188

Chapter 27

Never let a good crisis go to waste   193

Chapter 28

Brutal pandemic lessons   203

Chapter 29

Politics & the NYDA   210

Chapter 30

Breathing again   215

Chapter 31

Free to work   218

Chapter 32

Tough tender   224

Chapter 33

Fully untender   233

Chapter 34

Packing up   238

Chapter 35

London   242

Chapter 36

A global housing crisis   247

Chapter 37

'Focus!'   251

Chapter 38

G20 & a game-changing call   256

Chapter 39

The DigsConnect acquisition   263

Chapter 40

Shine on you crazy diamond(s)   269

Final thoughts   275

Acknowledgments   278

INTRODUCTION

I am not your typical overachiever. If there were a prize for "the girl most likely to fail", all indicators would point at me. If you had told any of my teachers at any point in my schooling career that I might amount to anything other than being sent to prison or at the very least being totally louche, they would have dropped dead in shock.

I was a precocious kid with too much energy and too much hope. I was far too needy in my quest for love. From a young age, I was told that I was naughty. I was told that I was disobedient. On all my school report cards, which my parents have kept to this day (God only knows why), it was the same old story for 12 years: "Claire (my old name) is highly disruptive in class. She refuses to be taught, she is troublesome, she is the only girl yet again to be awarded detention this term."

I hold the dubious honour of, at the age of five, being the youngest person in the history of my 100-year-old school to be sent to detention for telling the teacher she was stupid. By all accounts, she was.

Throughout my childhood, adults told me that I was a bad kid, so I started to act out that role. I didn't want to sit in class all day. I wanted to run around in fields, climb trees, read books I loved and not the set works. So, I did. I didn't want to do homework. I wanted to build forts. So, I did. I failed most tests spectacularly and was often placed in the last set.

Oftentimes, when I'm giving a talk or an interview and I'm asked about the founding story of DigsConnect, I refer to my childhood self and how much was stacked against me in terms of what "they" thought of me and who "they" told me I could be.

Steve Jobs once gave an iconic speech where he spoke about connecting the dots. This phrase has become folklore in startup circles. We all talk about "connecting the dots" – those big moments that almost drip with destiny. Of course, there are many other moments in the startup world that are less destiny-ish and simply mundane, filled with endless meetings to discuss sales optimisations. There are tax laws, and there are always those hundreds and hundreds of unread emails.

Some days it feels like you're in the utter toilet of destiny. On other days, it's watching seemingly everyone else in the entire startup world closing massive funding rounds with off-the-charts revenue while you can't seem to get your conversion rate right. It's standing at the end of the line and having no idea what's next, when there are no maps, no signs, no lights as you take your next step into the dark. It's the creeping thoughts of insecurity that maybe you're an impostor, that maybe you should be doing something else. It's having anxiety about the future but nevertheless choosing to stay in this murky land of who-knows-what and who-knows-why.

Growing up, I wanted to be a revolutionary. I imagined myself in the jungles of Central Africa and South America, or the mountains of Asia, or the deserts of the Middle East. I'd have an AK-47 strapped to my back and an assortment of warlord lovers, surrounded by a band of rebels, my army of chaos, calling out our defiance against The System, ready to dismantle it with our passion and bare hands.

Along the way, I found myself living in Camps Bay, practically neighbours with the president and driving a Mini (which I named Angela Merkel for reasons that will later become obvious). I dressed head to toe in adidas athleisure and had Tom Ford sunglasses perched on my nose. I was surrounded by my MacBook, iPhone, Aesop skincare range, soy-scented candles and pretentious yoga gear, with organic vegetables slowly steaming in my Smeg-fitted kitchen while my Spotify chill indie daily mix played through my Bose soundbar.

I'd wake up in my perfectly scented room under my white Egyptian-cotton duvet. Sometimes I'd think about my alter-ego rebel self, the Alexandria Procter who would have rubbed her eyes awake in a hammock in a rebel military base, and I'd feel a tinge of regret. Had I become a total sell-out? How had I landed here?

For the past two years, I've been living between London and South Africa. I sometimes spend time at the British Museum, diving in and losing myself in past civilisations, observing Gilgamesh, who lived forever, or Octavius, who spent his time empire-building. I often get carried away as I find myself consumed by Hannibal, marching elephants over the Alps, Rome in chaos; Cyrus destroying Babylon; Boudica leading an army; Genghis howling at the gate;

Shaka and the blood of the wizards; Joan of Arc burning at the pyre; and Cleopatra in her agony and ecstasy. These moments of uncanny bravery, of warrior hearts and the indomitable human spirit touch my heart deeply: when humans did the unimaginable, when for a moment in time they were celebrated or hated or idolised and then recycled as heroes in the great thermodynamic chain. Our line, unbroken. Our humanity, surviving always, somehow. All living on Sagan's Pale Blue Dot – fragile and precious beyond measure.

In the course of writing this book, I've been at sea several times, caught in the headlights by the sheer momentum of it all but somehow carried by my uncontainable energy and ebullience and always-say-yes attitude that whips me up in the gulf stream of everything happening around me. Sometimes, when the party ends, I don't know how to find my way back to the ground.

The thing about the ground is that gravity will pull you there whether you like it or not. So, one way or another, I land, crashing down, at times completely flattened by inertia, devoid of grace, to wash up on the shores of my consciousness. In the quiet of these moments, I finally remember *why*. Why humanity stands on distant shores and looks beyond the horizons and dreams of more. Why our greatness is defined by choosing to do the right thing, not when it's easy but when it's hard.

In *Pale Blue Dot*, Carl Sagan reminds us that despite all its material advantages, "the sedentary life has left us edgy, unfulfilled". In a way that only Sagan can, he tells us that nothing lasts forever and that it's beyond our powers to predict the future. He evokes a longing for the open road, which "still softly calls us", and he inspires us to be brave and discover "new worlds".

In *Moby-Dick*, Herman Melville speaks to all of us who are wanderers: "I am tormented with an everlasting itch for things remote. I love to sail forbidden seas..."

This is my story. This is the tale of a restless wanderer. This is the story of DigsConnect.

CHAPTER 1

LOVE SHACK

I am nearly 25 years old. I'm standing in the ancient, dilapidated former pottery studio with parts of the roof missing that now serves as the office of our startup, DigsConnect. We call it the "Love Shack", like in the B-52s song: *Love shack, baby, love shack.* The studio is about 700m down the road from the University of Cape Town (UCT), where my cofounder, Greg Keal, and I first met while doing our undergrad degrees.

Greg is a political friend – a "comrade", as 20-year-old South African champagne-socialist students all so nauseatingly call each other. That's before they grow up and realise that socialism only looks cool on Che Guevara T-shirts. Even though as students we believe we are all left of Mao, most of us are former private school kids and about as far from comrade status as Donald Trump.

It's February 2019, the hottest time of the year in Cape Town. Today, it's around 30 degrees Celsius. The sky is achingly blue. An army of bugs has declared war on us;

their droning reaches fever pitch in the hazy heat. The huge glass doors that are also our walls have all been slid open, so our office is more of a dodgy tin roof on struts than an actual building.

The Love Shack is fab in summer, a death-trap in winter, and often plays home to rats from Newlands Forest. On a highly memorable occasion, one of these huge rodents decides to hang out in our app developer Tristan's bag, only to be awoken rudely by a shriek from the depths of hell itself when Tristan discovers Monsieur Rat next to his beloved MacBook Pro 16-inch. In a Usain Bolt-like sprint, Tristan hurtles out the open doors, vowing never to return. We coax him back, after which he sits cross-legged on a chair so that his feet won't touch the floor. Somehow, he builds the entire DigsConnect app in lotus pose, and it goes to #1 on the App Store in South Africa the following year.

There's a document staring at us from one of the shitty hand-me-down desks plastered around the dingy room. It's a brand-new shareholders' agreement that's been sent to us by a group of Johannesburg-based financiers who want to invest in our year-old startup. Michael, our CTO, whom I had briefly dated before he joined Greg and me as cofounders, looks excited.

"You guys ready?" Greg asks as we stare at the document. There's a feeling in the air that our lives are about to change forever.

By now, we're all sweating, partly from the thick heat and still air and partly from the pent-up tension the document is eliciting. *Holy shit, is this real?* Outside, I hear the strains of "Looove shack, baby, looove shack!"

Dylan, Greg's boyfriend, is outside near the circle of tree stumps in the dirt field under the willow trees that doubles as our parking lot, canteen and late-night bush toilet. He's playing our song loudly on his phone and itching to crack open the cold beers.

It's all happened so quickly. We had initially aimed to raise R2 million in seed funding, which was very much in line with the seed rounds that were happening in Cape Town back in 2018. Instead of the hoped-for two bar, we now have a contract on the table with R12 million written all over it.

The following morning, I wake up feeling fantastic despite my room looking like a disaster. It always does. It's high summer in Cape Town and it's already sweltering. The sticky warmth of an African morning clings to you on a day when the sun is so bright it blinds you behind closed eyes, making you delirious, ecstatic, swooning with life's energy. My 25th birthday is just a couple of days away.

My phone lights up. The news of our R12 million DigsConnect deal is out. I'm flooded with messages, notifications and missed calls. Everyone is freaking out. Journalists are writing about it and trying to speak to me. I ignore all of them. Instead, checking the time, I realise I'd better collect the keys to my new apartment in Camps Bay, one of Cape Town's most sought-after suburbs along the Atlantic seaboard.

I have almost nothing to bring with me, having sold most of what I owned to put money into the business before we closed the investment round, so packing is easy. I slam my suitcase shut, give the middle finger to the tiny, crappy old apartment and chuck my bag into my car, Angela Merkel.

I blast the Rolling Stones, turn both windows down so that the wind can cool me down, and head into the city. After collecting the keys, I have to be at our office by 10am, so I need to hurry.

I turn up the music in the car. My hair's flying all over the place as the hot summer wind blasts through the open windows. I put my head out and yell as loud as I can, belting it out with Mick who's singing about "ridin' 'round the world" and "doin' this" and "signin' that". I have just become one of the youngest self-made female millionaires on the African continent. Holy shit!

CHAPTER 2

ADD ANOTHER ZERO

In November 2018, three months before "the big deal" comes through, we're working our arses off. Amid a whirlwind of pitches and flights across the country, word has trickled out about these kids in their early 20s who are fired up on their first startup with zero experience and quite possibly talking absolute bullshit with their hockey-stick graphs and insane projections but who are undeniably onto something with potential, something that has huge early traction. We're having fun.

Every moment of every day, we're delirious with the joy of building something unique. This kind of buoyancy and explosive energy can infect even the hardest-nosed of financiers.

Many important deals and inventions that have shaped our world happened behind closed doors, in private rooms and in closed circles. In our case, our startup is born in that sweltering, rat-infested Love Shack.

Weeks before the deal is signed, on one fine Thursday

morning in November 2018, we find ourselves sitting at a huge wooden table at a trendy co-working space in Green Point.

I've arrived early. I walk in through the huge glass doors leading to the open-plan space and sashay straight to the barista in the corner. "Decaf oat-milk flat white, please." I'm wearing high-waisted black yoga shorts, adidas superstar trainers and a white crop top with a watermelon on it that says "Reckless". I push my huge Tom Ford sunglasses up onto my head and look around, rolling my shoulders and stretching my back like a cat. It feels like I am in a movie, and the plot is epic. The sun streams in through the massive windows and the air smells like the ocean. I scan a QR code to pay for my coffee and make my way to a long table.

Sitting cross-legged on the wooden bench, I open my MacBook Air. I've been up until around 4am, working on another one of my crazy tangential ideas, this time for a feature called "The Virtual Res". The idea is based on the DigsConnect backbone but has applications more applicable to universities, government and bursary providers. (Years later, we will pitch this idea to the National Student Financial Aid Scheme in a tender bid to house hundreds of thousands of students. But that story comes later.)

My cofounder, Greg, joins me at the table. He is suited up and looking immaculate. Ever since our worlds collided back in 2014, he's radiated victory. When we first met at UCT, Uber had just launched in South Africa and was taking campuses by storm. Greg, being Greg, became the UCT Uber ambassador, signing up so many students that he accumulated enough Uber credits to arrive on campus every day in a black Mercedes-Benz saloon, wearing the requisite suit.

Greg is A-type to a T. He's that guy who used to retype all his homework in junior school so that it was perfect, handing it in one week early and reminding the teacher on the due date that homework had been assigned. I was the kid who forgot I had homework, who dashed to the bathroom to wing it and got water and food smeared all over the pages before finally handing in a dog's breakfast.

Greg is ordered; I am chaotic. Greg likes routine; I abhor it. Greg likes spreadsheets; I consider suicide at the mere thought of them. Greg likes conferences; I like art. But we are bound, almost by destiny it would seem, to make the world a better place on a massive and sustainable scale. We want to move humanity forward. And, of course, we also want to make some serious cheddar.

Greg's also a winner. While these are all marvellous traits, many other people have these qualities too. What gives Greg his edge, what makes him so remarkable, is that he is an extraordinarily good man. He has a heart of gold and the purest of souls. He is genuinely moved by human suffering – a compassionate being who wants to create good in the world and make this planet a better place. He's also got an epic sense of humour, which includes making loud farting noises with his mouth whenever I'm on phone calls nearby.

Greg looks at what I'm wearing. "Jesus Christ, your shirt literally says 'Reckless' and we're about to ask investors for millions of rand for our 10-month-old startup."

I grin widely. "You ready?"

"Are you?" he counters, sceptically. "I hope you've read through the budget and prepared."

"Preparation is for amateurs," I grin. "I have a gift. I speak from the heart, just like back in the SRC days, remember?"

"Oh my God, we are so fucked," he groans. He's begun to look slightly pale and peaky. I decide to hold back. Now is probably not the right time to test his nerves.

Greg tends to vomit under pressure. He is an absolute workhorse. He's always at his desk typing away furiously on his laptop or pacing in circles around the studio on a call, AirPods in his ears and downing his fourth or fifth coffee of the day, barking commands at anyone foolish enough to get within shouting distance. Even when we're racing off to a meeting, me behind the wheel of Angela Merkel, swerving manically around traffic because I've made us late again, he'll have his laptop out to squeeze in more work. When we're about to do a big pitch or some crisis has hit, he'll suddenly go pale and quiet, stand up and throw up spectacularly in the nearest and most convenient spot – a pot plant, out the window (very dangerous for passers-by when we are on the top floor), in our studio sink or in the dirt-road parking lot behind our studio. Then he'll calmly rinse his mouth, gargle and get back to work. It's quite remarkable.

One of Greg's most spectacular projectiles was when the news of our Money Drop at UCT broke in July 2018.

CHAPTER 3

DROPPING CASH

The DigsConnect Money Drop has become somewhat of a startup marketing parable in South Africa. It was a crazy idea at the time, but it worked. It's probably the one thing that got us our meetings with investors, secured the attention of the entire student base at UCT and indirectly helped us to get 10 000 beds listed just eight months after we launched our accommodation app.

In fact, the Money Drop may just be one of the jankiest publicity plots in startup history. (It definitely is one of the reasons why we're sitting at a table in Greenpoint, waiting for our potential funders to arrive.)

The idea is simple. Instead of doing the same boring marketing campaigns at UCT as a billion other vanilla companies, we decide to activate our brand by doing something crazy, something that will get us attention.

The challenges are considerable. We're a bootstrapped, six-month-old startup with zero money, no discernible team and no grasp of reality or the rule of law. The DigsConnect platform is dodgy on good days and completely broken on bad ones, hosted on a R30-a-month server and built by me (the self-crowned CTO at the time – Michael has yet to join DigsConnect) with knowledge accumulated from one year of computer science at UCT and a handful of YouTube tutorials.

What is deeply worrisome is that other student accommodation websites have started popping up all over the show as more and more people realise there is a student housing crisis and a sleeping monster of a market waiting to be served.

And so, in July 2018, we decide to break away from the pack using the only resources we have in abundance: energy, passion and our complete lack of *skaam* for our crazy ideas. For months we've been sitting in our little studio, swivelling around on our shitty chairs plucked from a junk sale, bouncing ideas off each other and scribbling them down on our whiteboard. By now, we've saved up R11 000. The time has come to put it to use.

Building a marketplace business is a perfect chicken-and-egg dilemma. You need sellers to sell to buyers, but sellers will only go where the buyers are. Buyers only go where there's the kind of stuff they want to buy from sellers. We've hacked our way to early traction by taking advantage of the fact that we're UCT students selling to other UCT students: our clients are ourselves, our friends, the guy sitting next to me in my maths lecture and the girl who's also studying in the library. The landlords are *our* landlords, and our "stock" are the houses that line the streets on our daily walk up to campus. And it really is *up* to campus: UCT is halfway up a bloody mountain – it's brutal walking there at 8am when you have a hangover.

So, while we've managed to get some good results, "good" is no longer cutting it. We want to be great.

Instead of spending the R11K on silly flyers that no one will read and which will invariably end up in trash cans, we decide to use R1 000 to print 1 000 stickers, courtesy of a local printer's special offer on licence-disc stickers – and throw the remaining R10 000 off the roof of a university building. That's our simple idea: chuck R10 000 in R10 notes up in the air, let the notes float around campus and see what happens.

The idea was born during an unplanned brainstorm on getting noticed. Once we had riffed off each other and spoken the plan into existence, we sat in the studio in stunned silence and then laughed hysterically. This idea was batshit, insane and probably illegal. It was everything that DigsConnect was about. We loved it.

Because this is all the money we have, we have to get strategic. No cocking around. We have to approach the exercise like a military operation. Greg is in his element, plotting furiously. Michael, who has by now come on board to rebuild the DigsConnect platform, is coding moodily in the corner, headphones on and throwing us dirty looks when we get too loud and disturb the peace.

First, we have to create a sense of expectation on campus. People must at least vaguely know what DigsConnect is. So, "phase 1" entails plastering the entire campus with our R1-a-piece, luminescent-pink DigsConnect stickers. They are tremendously sticky and most probably made of a highly toxic radioactive substance that I get all over my fingers and in my hair. (Worryingly, the residue leaves my fingers glowing slightly for a couple of days afterwards.)

By this stage, I have left UCT but still have my student card, so at the stroke of midnight, dressed in black and wearing a balaclava for added dramatic effect, I stealthily make my way to campus, creeping about like a Scooby-Doo villain.

When I was still studying at UCT, I campaigned for a seat on the SRC, the student governing body. I ran as an independent candidate with no political affiliation, so I campaigned alone and figured out the most strategic locations for posters, stickers and other branding material. Now I use this insider knowledge to my advantage as I move around like a cat burglar, plastering the entire campus with lurid pink DigsConnect stickers.

I sprint through shadows, dodge the sleepy security guards, avoid the cameras and leap over squeaky stairs. By dawn, the stickers are everywhere: on doors, posts, pillars, walls, seats and new coffee cups; underneath toilet seats and above urinals; adorning lecture-room walls; behind computer screens; on library shelves; in access-controlled staff rooms and science labs with specimens suspended in formaldehyde; inside textbooks; on every step up to Jameson Hall; and on all the tables in the UCT food court. I even slap one onto the forehead of a student who has fallen asleep at his desk in the 24-hour library.

To this day, there are still some of our stickers hanging around campus – ones in spots where they are almost impossible to remove. People still ask me how I got them there, but I will never tell. A magician never reveals her secrets.

Students walking around on campus see the name

"DigsConnect" everywhere. As an exercise in brand awareness, it's a hit.

The thing about startups is that it's not a question of resources; rather, it's a question of *resourcefulness*. "Do or die, there is no try."

Once the stickers have been up for a few days and general interest has been aroused, "phase 2" of the Master Plot is set in motion. There's a group of guys on campus who run a hilarious and wildly popular Instagram account of UCT memes. They have tens of thousands of highly engaged followers. I DM one of them to say, "We're going to throw R10 000 in ten-rand notes off a building at UCT. You guys wanna live-stream it?"

Thirty seconds later, I get the reply. "We're in."

On the morning of the Money Drop, the meme guys start posting teasers and stories about "something big" happening on campus at 1pm – at Jammie Plaza, which is the heart of the main campus. A buzz begins to ripple from lecture theatres to tutorial rooms. Within a couple of hours, it feels like the whole campus is electrically charged. I certainly am.

Meanwhile, Greg, Michael and I have arrived at UCT, wearing hoodies over our DigsConnect T-shirts so that no one will recognise us. We each have wads of cash hidden in our pockets, amounting to R10 000.

We innocuously make our way to the food court, where the lunchtime crowd has started to grow. The meme guys are hanging around, phones in hand and waiting for the big moment. Our emotions are at an all-time high. Greg and I are sweating bullets. Michael, who is going on his own route, has already thrown up twice in the bushes alongside the chemical engineering building (to mask the smell).

At the agreed time, Greg and I look at each other. We can already read each other's thoughts just from our facial expressions. We know this event could turn out to be carnage. We know it will be terrifying, that nothing will be the same after this, and that, if we pull it off, it will become one of the most important accomplishments in our startup's history. Deep breath. It's time.

We casually stroll into the food court. We shoot a glance at each other, rip our hoodies off and throw them aside. The Instagram guys begin recording from their strategic locations. Then we both scream: "FREE MONEY!" and throw fistfuls of notes into the air. I knew that the reaction would be fast, but not *that* fast. I can say with complete honesty that I now fully empathise with the springbok once the lion begins its assault. The onslaught from the lunch crowd is near-immediate as they storm us.

"Oh shit!" I think. I know I have to run. Greg and I speedily separate amid the chaos and fly out of the room like bats out of hell.

The Insta guys, meanwhile, are laughing hysterically and filming from all angles, while the number of viewers on their live-stream grows into the thousands as students across South Africa tune in. Word spreads like wildfire. A stampede follows us as we sprint out of the food court while chucking out bank notes with our flyers stapled to them. The mayhem intensifies. I lose sight of Greg, who has gone around the side of the mathematics block while I try to shake the crowd by going via the library. This is a mistake. Students breaking for lunch hear the screams of

"Free money!" and, quick as lightning, join the stampede and start closing in on me.

Genuinely terrified by the ravaging, Viking-like mob that I have whipped into a frenzy, I sprint down the stairs of the library, trying to get to Jammie Plaza where I hope I can make my escape. I burst through the double wooden doors and stop dead in my tracks, each hand grasping thousands of rand, as I face what seems like 5 000 students waiting for the big reveal. In what feels like a single orchestrated movement, they all turn towards me and eye the money I am clutching in my hands. A huge, haka-like roar erupts from the crowd. I know now that I am totally, completely and utterly fucked.

By this point, one of the Instagram guys has fought his way through the crowd and positioned himself atop the stairs of Jameson Hall. He captures some of the most iconic photographs of that day as I emerge from the library foyer and into the crowd.

Picture it: our glorious campus halfway up Table Mountain, a backdrop of blue skies and a blinding sun, a 25-year-old girl in a white DigsConnect T-shirt, and thousands of students roaring and raging and rioting. I run into the crowd and emit a war cry while I throw around money and enter a rugby-like scrum that would have brought a proud tear to François Pienaar's eye. In a monumental toss that could have won South Africa the World Cup 10 times over, I part with the last of the money, drop to my knees on the concrete pavement and crawl past the legs of the rioters to make my escape.

I then hear the crowd roar again as Greg appears at the other end of the plaza, throwing cash into the air like a ballerina. It rains down like confetti, a gift greater than manna in the desert for these cash-starved students in need of cigarettes and alcohol. The mood is electric, with people hanging out the windows from the nearby arts block to watch.

Once all the money has been "dropped", Greg and I try to make our way through the crowd to reunite with each other. The plaza is still buzzing, with whoops, cheers and laughter erupting. It feels like everyone is live-streaming on Twitter and Instagram, holding fistfuls of money and making their way to the food court where a huge feast of Coca-Cola and the shitty sandwiches that give us the runs is underway.

Greg, Michael and I finally link up in a dazed silence and make our way back up to the top of the campus. We jump into Greg's old silver VW Polo. Still shaking from the adrenaline, he drives (badly) back to the DigsConnect studio, stopping briefly at the Spar so we can buy a bottle of gin. Straight, no mixers. This is not a moment for dilution of any kind.

Back at the Love Shack, sitting on our desks, we make ourselves extremely strong G&Ts without the T. We turn on our phones and open our social media apps. Immediately, hundreds of notifications begin pinging: missed calls from journalists, articles on *Business Insider*, radio stations calling in, DigsConnect trending on Twitter, tagged posts on Instagram, and pics of the Money Drop inadvertently sponsoring parties, drinks and cigarettes for students across the campus and in Rondebosch, Observatory, Claremont and beyond.

The feedback is overwhelmingly positive. Traffic on the

DigsConnect platform soars to record levels on Google Analytics. That day, we not only win the Cape Town student housing market but also make national headlines. This catches the attention of our first-ever investors.

CHAPTER 4

INSTANT CHEMISTRY

The mood around the table is relaxed, open and pulsing with excitement and anticipation. It feels like magic.

Pitching is a lot like dating. You meet a stranger and share bits about your past and your hopes for the future. But most importantly, you feel out the chemistry. It's the same when it comes to pitching. Chemistry is everything. It's the feeling of being on the same page, understanding what the other party is saying and knowing they understand what you're saying – an alignment of vision, ethics, productivity, mindset and culture. There's an unspoken feeling of trust and a strange sense of recognition, almost a feeling of *déjà vu*.

The meeting with our very first investors has that all-transcendental chemistry. We just click. I often advise founders to stay away from investors for as long as possible because fundraising distracts you from your only real goal, which is to create value for your customers.

It's important to get your product market-pricing-fit and show profitability before running off and blabbing on about it. Casual chats with investors when you aren't crystal clear on what you need the money for are often a waste of time. Only once you can clearly show how the investment capital would fulfil your goal of value creation for your customers should funds be raised as quickly and concisely as possible. And then it's back to work.

Securing investment can be seriously frustrating, with few solid answers and weeks, if not months, of waiting just to get a reply. A clear "no" from an investor can actually be a blessing because then there's no wasting of precious time (although a clear "yes" is, of course, preferable).

With these investors, we somehow find common ground immediately. They are some of the good ones. In my usual no-filter style, I share every aspect of our business and we discuss the risks ahead. Greg and I are first-time founders, scarily young and what some would consider "dropouts" – Greg from his law degree and I from my science honours degree. But as business partners, we get on like a house on fire. We'd also worked together on projects while we were still at university.

It is probably clear as we sit in that room, pitching to these men who will become our first investors, that we both have a strong, clear vision for the future. We're two kids intent on winning, and our crazy passion must be shining through. These guys cut deals for a living – they've been doing it all day, every day, for years – so they know what they're looking for.

We tell them about our dream to create a product that will change the lived experience of millions of young people around the world. To reimagine what "home" means. To capture the magic of those intangible moments in your student digs with your flatmates, making coffee at 2am in the kitchen as you cram for the exams the next day, or having a braai on a Sunday afternoon with your future stretching ahead of you like an open road, longing to be explored.

We tell them that this feeling of togetherness, of community, of safety and security, of a base, a place to call home, is what DigsConnect will encapsulate. On a practical level, it will be a business where anyone who has invested in the South African economy and started a property portfolio will find tenants fast, fill up their buildings and keep reinvesting. Our vision is to bring people together to share spaces during those magical student years when they're halfway between childhood and adult life. We will bring students into neighbourhoods to breathe life into old and tired spaces. The students will in turn support local cafes, bars, theatres and bakeries, and revive communities with their youthful energy. And, perhaps most important of all, DigsConnect will play a key role in addressing the student housing crisis in South Africa. We tell them that we want to go global one day.

The meeting, like most first meetings with investors, was originally scheduled for half an hour, but we hold their attention for at least two hours. When it comes to its inevitable end, they stand up and one of them says: "Look, we're not going to waste anyone's time or fight over a few million rand. Our time is worth more than that. So, we're in."

We did not expect this response, but Greg and I share one of our telepathic looks and know to play it cool. I am usually the most uncontrollable, excitable and hyperactive person on the continent, but with that look, Greg is clearly saying, "For fuck's sake, play it cool, Proc!"

Then we all shake hands. The deal is done, and that is that.

The paperwork will follow, but all of us know that this is for real, that this is happening. In my experience, all the best deals or relationships start with the parties entering agreements based on their word and honour. I know straight away if I can trust someone. I felt it with Greg when I first I met him, and I feel it at the meeting with our investors.

"Wow, okay, fantastic!" I reply, trying to stop myself from gushing. "The ticket size is R2 million. How much of the round will you be taking?"

"We love the business. We'll be investing R12 million."

I shoot another quick look at Greg to see if we are in agreement. His look confirms it. I can hardly breathe. Twelve million rand!

"Alright. What are the timelines?"

"You can expect a term sheet in your inbox this evening, and the cash will be in the bank by the end of the month."

They settle the coffee bill and leave. A fleeting thought crosses my mind. Damn. If I'd known they'd be paying, I would have ordered food, seeing as I have only about R50 in my bank account. Then it hits me and I spin around to face Greg. "Did that just fucking happen?!" I yell, jumping up and down and shaking him like a madman. Greg, usually composed, is also freaking out.

"Okay, oh my God, what do we do now?" I scream.

"We grow this thing. It's time to make this massive." He looks like he's going to puke.

We exit the building and run around like maniacs, unable to control our laughter, bags swinging wildly, delirious and almost tripping over each other. We tumble into Greg's old, beaten-up silver Polo Vivo and play The B-52s as loud as we can, racing back to the Love Shack.

A couple of weeks later, after a bit of back and forth on the shareholders' agreement, we have the final draft. We stare at it lying on one of our cheap desks. It's a cooking hot February day in Cape Town, and all the sliding doors (which are also our walls) are open. The air is thick with the buzz of bugs in the bushes and trees, creating a symphony in the background. I tie my long blonde-brown hair into a messy bun to stop it from sticking to my skin. I'm barefoot again – my shoes are on the grass outside – and I'm using my little green summer dress to fan my legs.

We click open our pens, and our office intern puts on a blow-up T-rex outfit just for the hell of it. In unison, we take a breath and sign the shareholders' agreement.

The photo from that day shows the founders of what will become the biggest housing app on the African continent, signing the contract with a T-rex standing in the corner. It perfectly sums up the DigsConnect culture.

And with that single piece of paper, at 25 years old I officially become CEO of DigsConnect and one of Africa's youngest self-made millionaires. (As a woman, I might have even held the top spot.)

"Right, well, back to work, I guess," says Greg.

I sit back down at my shitty desk, take a sip of coffee and get back to it. It's February 2019, and our lives have just changed in unimaginable ways.

41

CHAPTER 5

FROM DROPOUT TO FLYING HIGH

It has taken us just over a year since I launched my rudimentary version of DigsConnect to land this well-publicised R12 million investment. At the time, it's the largest seed round in South Africa ever, and my two partners and I are all under the age of 25 and first-time cofounders.

Overnight, I go from being an underperforming varsity dropout with wildly idealistic dreams and nothing but burning passion to my name to being the co-owner of a kickass tech startup.

What follows is a slew of publicity, hyper-growth in our user numbers and listings across the entire country, rapid scaling of operations and recruiting of expensive engineers and team members. We haven't quite figured out what the core product will be, but we have a million ideas that we keep tacking on, so the sheer momentum of it all feels like progress. (As a side note, I would explicitly not recommend this approach now that I know better. My advice would be to first lock down your model and traction before scaling the team and overheads.) And while we don't have much of a business model, we do have a system whereby our users will pay every time we offer a different type of service. Serendipity (and chutzpah) has positioned us as unique founders in our market, segueing between landlords and students. We ride that wave ferociously to get early and fast results for our users.

Night and day, our nail-bitingly young and indefatigably explosive team sits in a circle, facing each other and armed with whiteboard markers, to throw around ideas. Then I jump up and write it all on the walls and windows and desks of our dilapidated little Love Shack office. I manically draw connecting lines between all the ideas, and somehow the graphs always seem to point up and to the right.

We feed off each other's energy and genius and untameable optimism. No frontier is too remote, no idea too risky, no campaign too audacious. I mean, we are the crazies who chucked thousands of rand off rooftops at UCT, generating a media frenzy and locking down our core market in just three hours. We're on a mission to change the world, and the world thus far seems pleased to have us. All these pulsing ideas are quickly thrown into technical production. We spin up features in a matter of hours and launch them immediately with almost no testing, often causing the site to crash. "Technical debt", "QA" and "staging servers" are words we don't even know yet.

I have zero management experience (other than those wanky leadership training programmes for prefects and student leaders). When it comes to real life, where you suddenly find yourself leading a team of hyper-intelligent engineers and salespeople, the theories go out the window, and you just have to go in with every ounce of your authenticity. Added to that, I have no business knowledge (I can't even spell the word "entrepreneur"). I have never managed a budget, let alone a spreadsheet.

These are "my salad days, when I was green in judgement, cold in blood". Thank you, William Shakespeare.

On top of it all, the guy who I'd been dating (albeit briefly) has become our new CTO. Things are still a bit awkward between us. Greg and I knew we needed a technical cofounder, so when Michael asked to join us, he and I decided to call it quits romantically and rather focus on being cofounders. Again, this is something I would not recommend to anyone going into business. You can be two of the most rational, kind and ambitious individuals, but these sort of feelings are complex and the added distraction is not welcome in the early days of a startup.

As much as I want to believe that I have the credentials of a Startup Goddess because I've read Peter Thiel's manifesto, *Zero to One*, a couple of times, I don't know shit. Before you have faced your first crisis, adapted, stood your ground and overcome a slew of challenges, you hardly even qualify as a Startup Flea. Nonetheless, as green as we are, we are rocketing in the best way possible.

There's this indescribable feeling that happens when you go from being lost in the wilderness of your youth to the sudden realisation that you've found your path, that you've found your meaning, that you've finally found what you're meant to do with your life – and, what's more, that you've found the people you'll be doing it with. You've found how you can contribute to this crazy, terrifying and wonderful exploration of our civilisation. You've found a way to keep carrying forward all that's been done in the past. You've found that when it comes to testing whether you're worthy, you can fight and run when you're thrown into the ring – not even to get to the finish line but simply because you love the feeling of it. That the best moments of being human are when you're trying really fucking hard at something that you believe in. That the meaning is in the struggle because that's what gives it its worth – trying really hard. That everything that exists around us in this world is simply there because some crazy person or small group of people decided that they would not give up trying until they had built that "thing". And that *now* is your chance to take a shot because, in the end, I believe that humans are made to stand at the frontiers, look further, create and build.

Overnight, I have literally woken up to find that the future I have dreamed of for the world will be the result of me building it. And if I'm going to be all hand-wavey about it, quasi-Buddhist-millennial even, I can say that it all feels like fate. At the same time, it is pure chaos, and we don't even realise just how chaotic it will become until we're so deep in it that it's impossible to get out.

But in these early days of naive passion, where everything is possible, it feels like we're onto something big, as if we're navigating our way through it all on our rocket ship. We have even called our core strategy document "The DigsConnect Rocketship Manual". It makes me feel like a child again, not weighed down by the complacency of others who try to dissuade you from taking a risk; like

a child with no knowledge that some things might hurt;
like a child when the world opens up before you and gets
more and more wonderful with every corner you turn. In
that state of mind, it feels like anything is possible.

CHAPTER 6

BORN (NEARLY) FREE

I was born on a Sunday evening in 1993, just after *Carte Blanche* with Derek Watts and co and right before the 8 o'clock movie. It was the year before South Africa held its first democratic election in which Nelson Mandela was elected as our president. For South Africa, it was an auspicious year. My birth, however, was a fairly ordinary event.

To a world of 5.548 billion human beings, one more was added: a baby girl, born Claire Jean Procter. From as early as I can remember, people would tell me that Claire was a pretty name. I never liked it. A name isn't necessarily one's destiny, but what one believes about oneself is. I didn't want to be pretty. I wanted to be great. At the age of 15, I would officially change my name to Alexandria, inspired by Alexander the Great.

The town I made my first yell in, Port Elizabeth, now called Gqeberha, is the biggest city in the Eastern Cape, which is the most poverty-stricken rural province in South Africa. Coincidentally, it's also where Mandela hailed from.

Gqeberha is wedged between two bays. When you drive into the city from the east, it's perched small and squat in the dusty and dry ruggedness of the rural Eastern Cape. The potholes are numerous and ginormous. Cows and livestock wander around in the streets.

If you come in from the western side, the city reveals its more picturesque parts, and you can sort of understand why so many of the Europeans who washed up here decided to stick around. Some of the older streets are lined with Victorian cottages that date back to the 1820 settlers. It is from these settlers that I am partly descended. The other side of my South African heritage runs back much further to the 1600s and the Dutch traders and farmers who brought their ships and guns and germs to the Cape of Good Hope, also known as the Cape of Storms. Their arrival caused a ripple effect that would be felt through the country for centuries.

The story of my ancestors can be seen through two lenses. On the one hand, it is quite grim, as is any history when viewed through the lens of modernity or colonialism. On the other hand, it is a story of incredible endeavour. Humans arriving on foreign shores with nothing but their wits and resilience and each other to rely on, forging a new life. I understand this is contentious. In tales of fortitude, one group often succeeds at the expense of another. Human history is a story of persecution, of injustice, of cruelty, of rape and of subjugation. But I try to relate to the murky waters of our past by understanding it at the level of the individual and in their context. I'm drawn to the story of the young Xhosa boy and what he had to do to survive, of the Boer wife and what she had to do to survive.

Humans are wonderfully ubiquitous, and my travels around the world have led me to having incredibly diverse conversations. Along the way, I've discovered that most people, whether they're in Kinshasa or in New York City, essentially want the same thing. People want to be happy, to fall in love, to do something meaningful with their lives, to feel safe, to feel free, to laugh often, to eat well, to have a cosy home and to be part of a loving community.

I grew up on a smallholding, about 20 minutes outside Gqeberha and close to a beach called Sardinia Bay. Sundays at Sards were a tradition. We were salt-soaked and sunburnt, catching waves on our boogie boards, my brother and I usually fighting as we tried to share a foot-long hotdog from the WurstWagon that was (and still is) parked in the Sardinia Bay parking lot.

My childhood home, Lothlorien, was a huge, soaring grey mass atop the highest hill in the region, commanding a sweeping view of the rolling hills, all the way down to the vast, blue Indian Ocean that stretched from left to right. My bath was on the western side of the house and looked out over all of this. Most evenings, I would lie there for hours reading books and journals, ignoring my never-completed homework, with death metal on my CD player and the bath water turning from lobster-red-skin-inducing hot to tolerable, warm and then cold while the colours of the sky and the trees outside changed.

The sun set to the west of the *stoep*, over Jeffreys Bay and St Francis Bay. When the huge sky lit up, it rippled in a blaze of red, orange, purple, magenta, blood, fire, famine, void and glory.

Then there were the morning thunderstorms. I'd wake

up early when the warm rain splattered through my always wide open windows onto my sleeping face. There I'd lie, cosy and slightly sticky under my always too-thick duvet. Sometimes I'd stand up to close the windows and watch the tropical rain as it lashed down. The air was thick and wet in those rainy months before it turned dry and parched, when the grass became yellow and shrivelled up and the concrete walls of the houses and the tin roofs of the shacks burnt to the touch. These were the months when the dogs lay heavily on the driveways and panted, tongues out and drooling. It was a time when the annual summer water restrictions came into effect and my dark brown hair turned blonde in the sun. The smell of meat cooking on the braai lingered in the air.

Behind the house was rugged bushveld inhabited by buck and bushpig and the occasional baboon. There were other smallholdings and hectares of farmland dotted all around, and in front of it all lay the ocean.

We had horses and, after school, I'd saddle up Major Doo, my trigger-happy and completely psychotic ex-racehorse, and go careening through the veld. He was prone to bucking and bolting. I'd have a hell of a good time when he shied and took off at a hundred miles an hour over farmland and fences and the occasional cow. I would usually stay in the saddle when he became possessed, but on one occasion, he threw me spectacularly into an acrobatic somersault, breaking my left ankle in the process. I had to remount all 16 hands of him (not easy with a broken ankle) and ride home because cellphones weren't really a thing in those days. Thank God he didn't run off too far. I like to think he was plagued by guilt at having inconvenienced me, so he meekly took me back home to be carted off to hospital (yet again).

I'm the kind of person who unfortunately attracts these kinds of events, and as a child, I was a regular at the emergency room. At 13, I was bitten by a lion (a baby one, admittedly, but a lion – *Panthera leo* – in all its mighty, bloodthirsty majesty). At 11, I did a trial run on the neighbourhood kids' homemade zip-line, and when it (predictably) got jammed halfway down the incline, I was thrown about 30 metres and blacked out on impact. This was South Africa, though, so no one really took this stuff too seriously. "Walk it off and don't be a wimp" was the way of our world. I happily cycled home with my brother afterwards, and we enjoyed an episode of *Pokémon* while eating a favourite meal we had created called *gommie* (with a guttural Dutch "g"), which was essentially sugar on bread crushed under a chopping board into a flat pancake and eaten by the loaf-load.

Falling out of trees, accidentally swallowing rose poison, getting mauled by the occasional dog, slamming fingers in car doors, completely chopping off a finger, jumping out of cars, breaking windows, nearly drowning after being caught in a riptide, and, my *coup de grâce*, flipping my dad's twin-cab bakkie on a dirt road one week after getting my licence, completely wrecking it and then hopping out of the wreckage with a flourish of the metaphorical hat and without a scratch (and no seatbelt) – all of these are kind of my brand. I call it the Jack Sparrow effect.

I must at this point state, for the record, that I am 100% the victim in these events, and in no way do I try to inspire or encourage this chaos. I always think I can pull it off, and, well, I usually (kinda) do, minus the odd severed finger here and there. But that's why we have spares. All I need is one finger to point commandingly at stuff, and the rest really are excessive. I'm a yes-by-default person, a "we can 100% do this" person, a "what a ride!" person, usually dragging along horrified bystanders into the intensity of my full-volume existence.

I vividly remember our sprawling country house, with the hordes of dogs and horses and chickens and hamsters and endless parties and friends and passions. Those hot African summer evenings with the Christmas beetles and cicadas. School holidays that lasted several lifetimes. Every door flung open to catch the breeze, and the thick, double-volume silk curtains billowing out when the wind caught them. Gin bottles everywhere. Swimming costumes drying on the deck. Drunken adults racing home after dinner parties, roaring "The country's going to the dogs!" over the shrieks of the kids as the "grownups" sped down the driveway, taking out half the rose bushes to my mother's horror and narrowly missing the dog. The troupe of kids running wild over the lawns, waging war with each other. Barefoot and breathless. The chandeliers were all blazing, and there was always rock 'n roll music.

To me, my childhood felt typical. All the kids at my school had kinda the same set-up, so for us this was normal.

The perfect and devastating emblem of this was little baby Claire strapped to the back of her Xhosa nanny, Sunna, as she sang to me on our long walks under the acacia trees. Almost all my photos from my childhood are of me in her arms or strapped to her back. I can't remember the words to the songs, but occasionally as an adult I'll hear the melodies again and I'll want to cry – not from sadness or happiness, but for what has been. My tears wish to mark her life and my life and the years she spent holding me. My world was the cocoon of the blankets strapped to her body. Knocking on her door in the middle of the night after a nightmare, knowing she would always come for me. We little white babies of Africa. How complex, this South Africa of ours!

Back then, I was too young to be uneasy about notions of inequality or political machinations. I wandered around outside, always bored, sprinting up, waving and whooping at the gardener – his endless patience and kind smile, teaching me the wonders of nature, showing me flowers blooming and watching the bees gathering pollen in rapture and delight, and my total and utter ignorance of what my very existence meant in the fraught early days of our national democracy. As a child, I had no idea of the system that was being perpetuated.

At this point, it must be said that memoirs can be treacherous. There are murky grounds to navigate. We usually look back on the past with more knowledge and insight than what we had when those events transpired. Especially when we were children. We watch the world of adults and injustice, our innocence guarded only by inexperience. In our own lives, we are almost always overwhelmed by complexity, and when you add the complexities of the billions of lives around us, those we interact with directly and indirectly, we realise that our lives often stand on a knife's edge between devastating and beautiful.

I was born with a spoon of stubborn idealism firmly planted in my mouth.

I am just about as old as our democracy; the Mandela generation, the born-frees, the beleaguered millennials who have to reconcile every wrong perpetuated on every previous generation, which weighs heavily on our shoulders. We understand implicitly that if we don't make it work, it would have all been for nothing.

Milan Kundera said that "in the sunset of dissolution, everything is illuminated by the aura of nostalgia, even the guillotine". We are in so, so many ways the product of context. And where we are scattered and take root, we must come to terms with our place in the world, our place in time, our duties and our destinies, should we have the courage to seize them.

I often think of the unbroken line stretching back from myself, generation upon generation, across continents, millennia, aeons and species, changing form but always a single thread, right up to an inception point. A first breath. We're not as far from each other as we sometimes think we are. Or are told we are. I often remind myself of this birthright to exist. Because I, too, have a bloodline of ancestors somewhere out there in the dust.

CHAPTER 7

PRACTICAL PETE & THE GREAT HEID

My dad is Peter, known to many as Dr Peter Procter. We call him "Practical Pete" or "Volcano Pete" or "The Turtle". These are apt nicknames. Padre is a dermatologist who is known throughout the Eastern Cape for treating much of the collective teenage acne in the province (which paid for my school fees).

Practical Pete's idea of a great Christmas present is a torch, a Leatherman, a windbreaker, one of those keychains that is actually a tightly wound rope that can be used in an emergency, or a Thermos bottle that keeps the liquid inside either cool or hot. That gift was one of his big hits. To this day we have thousands of them stacked in our kitchen. What did I tell ya? He's a helluva practical guy.

My dad is also one of the coolest people I know. He always has a great book or a band to recommend to me. Now that I've hit my 30s, I can 100% confirm that he's my best friend. We speak every single day. I mostly call him in the evenings, when he's done seeing patients at his practice and before he heads off to the hospital. He works insane hours and has hardly any free time, but he always takes my calls or calls back within the hour. He is rock solid when it comes to being dependable. No matter how tired he might be, he is always there.

He's helluva awkward around emotions and he pretty much has no idea how to handle my all-encompassing intensity. But his grounded presence, combined with one of his brilliantly funny comments, can diffuse the worst parts of my extreme nature.

Practical Pete had the remarkable fortune of finding a career that he really loved, but it was in fact my fierce grandmother, Audrey Procter, who picked it for him.

Audrey was a hoot. She was a hell of a woman. Her first marriage was at 19. Five children and 20 years later, she became a widow. It was then that she met Leslie Procter, an Englishman born in Penang, raised in Sussex and schooled in Dulwich who graduated from Cambridge University. He had, like most of the men from his generation, fought in WWII. After the war, he worked in marketing in London and sailed the Med. Nicknamed "The Spaniard" because of his sailing tan, he arrived in South Africa when he was 60. She was 40. They met, quickly married, and a year later out popped baby Peter.

Volcano Pete is usually a remarkably chilled guy – dormant, if you will – but he will eventually blow his top in epic proportions. One such memorable occasion was Christmas 2018. All the kids had left the old homestead for their own digs, so Practical Pete was used to having a surgically clean house and kitchen, just the way he liked it. Everything was in its allocated, often labelled, place.

At Christmas, we all descended on the house like Genghis Khan's invading hordes, bringing along boyfriends and friends and stragglers. Now, something you should know about me, and this might shock you, is that I wouldn't be classified as neat and orderly. Within five minutes of arriving anywhere, general chaos and disorder surround me. I don't even know how it happens. Scientists should study it, actually, because if it could be bottled, it would be a great weapon of mass destruction. (In 2023, while staying with a friend on a trip to India, I caused utter hilarity for his entire family when they saw that, within an hour of my arrival, I'd turned my room into the sort of scene that rivalled the Great Mumbai Outdoor Laundry, only with less order.)

Anyway, back at the homestead for La Navidad, one morning my sister Kate and I knocked up a humongous breakfast worthy of several Michelin stars, destroying Pete's pristine kitchen in the process.

After feasting, we retired to the lounge in a food coma and tried to recover by helping ourselves generously to Practical Pete's liquor cabinet. (It's never too early for a cheeky prosecco in December in South Africa.) Good old Practical P entered stage left, a grim look clouding his face as he surveyed his usually spotless kitchen that was now transformed into a crime scene. We (meaning my sister) would clean it up eventually after I'd bribed her sufficiently to pick up my share of the housework. (Business lesson 101: everyone has a price.) However, Practical P, who abhors a mess, got down to business immediately. After a solid hour of cleaning, the job was done and he exited stage right, somewhat perturbed but nonetheless with his heart at peace. By this time, I'd recovered sufficiently and was in dire need of a good coffee. I made for the kitchen but couldn't quite decide if I wanted filter coffee with the plunger or the stovetop coffee that usually boiled over on my watch. So, I decided to make both. I happily poured myself a cup, put on my bikini and dreamily retreated to the pool for a bit of poolside philosophising.

Practical Pete came back into the kitchen and saw the offending coffee pots and rings of coffee slowly staining the kitchen counter. Unimpressed, patience wearing thin, he mopped it up and cleaned the plunger. With a heavy sigh, he retired to his study. My sister then went to the kitchen and made a new pot of filter coffee before joining me at the pool. Two minutes later, we heard a scream of pure anguish as Practical P entered the kitchen for the third time, only to see, once again, a mess. The man could only be pushed so far, and with that, he grabbed the coffee plunger and flung it clear over the back wall, never to be seen again. RIP filter coffee for the rest of the day. Vesuvius had erupted in all its glory. After that, with order restored, like a volcano, he returned to a state of dormancy. Kate and I ran and hid, trying to quell roars of laughter. Within the hour, I'd gone on Takealot.com to order another plunger, scheduled for urgent delivery.

During all of this, my mother was nowhere to be seen. What can I say about Mummy dearest? Oh boy, oh boy, oh boy. Maybe I'll start with her nickname, which is close to an executive summary. Advocate Heidi Vanessa Shelver Procter, more commonly known as "Heartless Heidi", or "The Great Heid" – the unofficial leader of Gqeberha who calls the mayor(s) on an hourly basis, barking out orders and keeping the municipality on a tight leash. Madre is the ultimate puppet master who keeps us all dancing to her tune.

Heartless Heidi comes from less glamorous stock than Practical Pete. Her parents certainly weren't sailing the Med when they met. However, good old Heartless H is a real tiger and was never one to accept her lot in life. She won a scholarship to study law, ran with it to become an advocate and state prosecutor in Pretoria appointed by the minister of justice, and eventually opened a family law clinic back in old Port Elizabeth.

While I was growing up, my mother and I would have explosive stand-offs, in near-gladiatorial style. She was a fantastic opponent. Learning how to outwit her at a tender age steeled my nerves for many future battles – which included twice defending myself in court after being sued, and winning both times. Now as an adult, I'm able to see her as a human being, and I realise how remarkably privileged I am to have this fierce, never-say-die woman as a mother. She is the original Upstart.

CHAPTER 8

AN EDUCATION

"Your daughter is trouble." I'm five years old and sitting in the headmaster's office, again, with my parents on either side of me. I'm wearing my St George's Preparatory School uniform, which comprises a white collared shirt, red pinafore, black school shoes and white socks. My knees are scuffed, as always, and my hair is wild and probably has a twig or two in it. My mom looks bored. My dad looks harassed.

I'm on the brink of expulsion, yet again. This time for telling a teacher that she's a brain-dead mouth-breather. This is simply a fact. When I tried to explain to her why my argument was superior and why she wasn't fit to instruct me, instead of receiving the humble apology I was expecting, I was sent to detention and warned to toe the line or else. Anyway, neither she nor the headmaster saw the truth or humour in the situation.

"I'm sure it's not that bad," my father tries to ease the situation.

"Dr Procter, your daughter is the youngest person in the history of our school to go to detention! In Grade 1! At five years old! This school is over 120 years old!" the headmaster splutters in despair.

Look, my timing probably wasn't spectacular. I could have spaced it out a bit more. The previous week's offence that had led me to his office was my purported insolence towards the sports teacher. She was the pits. A regular Mrs Trunchbull in the purest sense of the word. *"I'm right, you're wrong; I'm big, you're little."* I saw how her hands itched to grab me by the pigtails and fling me out the window and over the rugby fields after she saw me carving my made-up family crest (consisting of dragons and sea monsters) into an ancient wooden school desk. She certainly didn't encourage my artistic impulses.

Mr van der Hoven, the headmaster and an ex-Rhodesian, wasn't a bad guy. He often indulged me and was usually on my side when I was sent to his office. He would plonk me down on the massive leather wingback armchair in his oak-panelled office and pace in despair. "You're the smartest girl in the class. Why don't you act like it?"

I'd get up, grab some sweets from the jar on his desk and divert the conversation to something more interesting, like a story I had seen on the news.

Back in the office with my parents still deep in discussion about the detention fiasco, I can see out the window that break has just started. My friends (the most mischievous boys in the grade, who also serve as my henchmen in my plots of chaos, which may or may not include the odd firecracker in a toilet) are outside playing foursquare, a game where you hit a tennis ball with your hand between four squares. I'm the reigning champion and not about to miss a game. It's time to get this show on the road. So, I decide to pull the oldest trick in the book. At an early age, I've learnt the power of switching on the waterworks.

I begin to cry. Sobs and blubbers. I am transformed into a picture of shame and compliance. I show all the repentance of a sinner who crawls through the desert on her knees for 40 days and 40 nights seeking absolution. Ten minutes later, after surreptitiously wiping my crocodile tears on the sleeve of my pinafore, I am destroying my competition on the foursquare court.

Many detentions later, my days at St George's Preparatory School ended and my time as a boarder at the Diocesan School for Girls in Grahamstown began. This is where I decided to change my name.

I had already discovered the wonders of the internet at an early age and trawled it endlessly on our home computer or on the decrepit computer in the common room at boarding school. I plunged into all the information and knowledge available and found inspiration for my name change. I delved into the tales of historical figures I could relate to, and I read books with concepts that blew my mind. I watched films with ideas that blew it even more. I was and still am drawn to all manner of stories that embrace brave, true and clean endeavours, that cross frontiers, which speak of vicious freedom. Back then, I realised that the type of person I wanted to be wasn't out of reach and that others had followed their crazy ideas to incredible conclusions. Surely it would also be possible for me?

Once I had chosen my new name, Al-ex-an-dri-a (a name with five syllables), I wrote it out on the back of a school notebook. Alexandria sounded cool and alluded to my interest in Alexander of Macedonia, in the Pharos, in the library, in the ancient city. For a second name, I choose Syrah in reference to Cyrus II of Persia, whose rule and conquests inspired Julius Caesar.

(After more than a decade, my parents and extended family have still not adjusted to my name change.)

I would discover some time later that my mother had in fact wanted to call me "Alexis" before I was born, while my father had wanted to call me "Sarah". Their compromise was "Claire". I am convinced I have made the right choice: Alexandria Syrah Procter.

By the time I'd settled on what I would officially be called, I was 14 and ensconced at a boarding school in a tiny town at the bottom of Africa. On the day, it felt like something in my life had irrevocably and profoundly changed.

From the moment I changed my name, it reinforced my love for rebellion and my attitude of "if I don't like it, I will change it, and you cannot stop me". It was a life-changing decision to take responsibility, guide my own ship and decide my own fate.

I had wanted to do this for a long time, and despite everyone saying no – my parents, the teachers, even the law (I was a minor) – I found a way and did it anyways. By changing my name, I became master of my own destiny. I realised that my only duty on earth was to recreate truth from first principles, accept nothing and build the world in my highest vision. In my idealistic, anything-is-possible adolescent mind, I wanted to take responsibility for the future of humanity and consciousness in our expanding universe. I could see that the future was nothing more than what we made it.

We have to decide what we want it to be, and then we just have to do it. I know it is up to me to fashion the life I want for myself, and in creating a beautiful world, I will elevate the lives of others – a rising tide of progress and flourishing humans.

My new name gives me the courage to fight the system. But I am 16, at an incredibly privileged boarding school, living a remarkably comfortable life. What do I know about injustice?

As the name of my school, Diocesan School for Girls, suggests, it is built around a chapel and church services are mandatory for students – hence I try to stage a protest for religious freedom. It is a resounding failure because no one turns up to protest with me. My only reward is a month of detention and having to write an apology letter to the reverend. My timing is probably off, as the previous week I was protesting to save Darfur. I even reused the same placard, so the back read "Save Darfur" and the front "Religious freedom now!". A couple of weeks later, I add "End female genital mutilation NOW" under "Save Darfur", and the mixed messaging may be part of the reason why I fail to garner support. However, my efforts do not go unnoticed.

One Sunday evening, as we're finishing chapel, I get up from the pew and began to file out with the other girls when I feel a tap on my shoulder. I turn around and see Isabella, an older girl, standing in front of me. She is without a doubt the smartest girl in the school. She is famously doing 10 subjects (the norm is seven) and acing them all. She was offered the much-coveted honour of prefecthood but rejected it in front of the entire school. It was an iconic moment when she walked on stage and turned down the much revered "golden girdle". I know her vaguely, as she is a member of the tiny debating league to which I also belong. She is also a grounded, unpretentious and hell of a nice person with a great sense of humour who will end up working for Google in Silicon Valley and creating some of the software powering their self-driving cars.

"Procter," she says. "I have something for you." She hands me an envelope with my name written on it: Alexandria Procter, Espin House, Grade 10. "If you have any questions, we can chat after dinner." She turns and joins her friends who are waiting for her at the door of the chapel.

I stand frozen, expecting the worst. I am constantly on the verge of expulsion. I think about all the rules I have broken recently and wonder what evidence they have against me, and how I will concoct my defence. A handwritten letter is a strange way of delivering the news that I have been expelled. Perhaps I am being extorted? How exciting. Finally, something worth thinking about amid the dreary drudgery of high school. At last, an enemy worth my while! I hope the plot is devious and worthy of an epic counterplot.

Still standing in the dim and sanctified light of the chapel, I flip the envelope over and slide a finger under the flap, trying not to rip it. I rip it anyway. "Crap," I mumble under my breath. I pull out the folded letter.

Alexandria Procter,
You have been selected to join the Alchemists' Philosophical Society.

The Alchemists' Society is a secret, invitation-only society for DSG and St Andrew's College students who uphold curiosity, freedom of thought and expression, scholarly debate and witty repartee.

Our members are selected in Grade 11, yet every year one member is selected in Grade 10. Early entry comes with a responsibility. You will lead the society next year and are expected to contribute more to the maintenance of the society.

If you accept this invitation, please avail yourself at our next rendezvous next Sunday evening at Mr Braithwaite's house. You must prepare a philosophical paper on an idea that has been plaguing you recently, which you will present to the rest of the society for discussion.

Yours,
The Alchemists

"Holy shit!" I say.

The reverend of the chapel shoots me a look of outrage with eyes full of Old Testament judgment. I am already past my last chance with her after bunking chapel with religious fervour. (On one memorable occasion, I was found sitting in my cupboard with a torch, a copy of *The*

Catcher in the Rye and a pilfered packet of the teachers' common-room tea biscuits. I was covered in crumbs and wild-eyed from shock as she tore open the cupboard door and yelled "PROCTER!". It also certainly hadn't helped our fractured relationship that I went on Rhodes University radio to say that being forced to go to chapel when I was a practising Buddhist impinged on my religious freedom. The interview caused an uproar.)

So, clutching my envelope, I hot-tail it out the back door of the chapel. Once I am alone, I read the letter again. I then head to the library to start working on my first paper. I pick a lighthearted topic: the nature of consciousness. I am 15 years old and gloriously ignorant.

Time does its own thing, and we grow up. The next thing I know, I am 17 and weeks away from finishing my high school career. It is November in Grahamstown, the last month of spring, the last month of school and the end of 12 years of formal private-school education.

The end feels like the sound of cicadas in the evenings, of the chapel bell ringing to mark the time between classes. It is the smell of dust on old wooden floors. It is the feeling of names scratched into schoolroom desks and running your fingers over the carved grooves; an audible echo of the thousands of feet walking these same paths, books under arms, for hundreds of years; the same trivial concerns about boys and being misunderstood; and pangs of concerns for this entity called The Future. It is the indignation of knowing in your heart that you're always right and that the adults are simply misguided. It is the confidence of ignorance.

Two months after finishing my last exam, at the age of 17, I board a one-way flight to Mumbai.

CHAPTER 9

FROM INDIA WITH LOVE

I finish high school in 2010. Having placed somewhere among the top 40 students in the national English Olympiad, I am awarded a scholarship to study at Rhodes University in Grahamstown. My parents are thrilled that I have passed and not, instead, been arrested. Their joy quickly turns to horror when I inform them that I have turned down the scholarship and will go backpacking solo through India. My goal is to circumnavigate the globe – thanks to Jules Verne, another firm favourite.

I am 17 and gloriously sanctimonious. I'm convinced that somewhere out there, I'll find the meaning of life, that I'll find all the answers and some kind of peace of mind. I'm consumed with the idea of getting to the root of human suffering, whatever that's supposed to mean. Maybe I'm just trying to get away from my parents.

So, in January 2011, when everyone from my matric year starts their first year at university bright-eyed and bushy-tailed in their quest to become a version of their parents, who are in turn versions of *their* parents, I go in search of Life.

The dreary insipidness around me has been driving me crazy. Are we all making it up? Are we all pretending to fit into this make-believe world? It feels like everyone around me is faking it, participating in an inane ritual without context or pleasure, following rules for the sake of it and only experiencing stagnation. I can't stand it. What is everyone so scared of that they are willing to give up their independence? What is this omnipresent myth that everyone is kowtowing to? It feels like everyone is jumping on conveyer belts to get whipped into detergent-buying, spin-class-attending, complacency-dating, car-insuring, airline-miles-collecting, never really feeling or doing or being much other than feeding with bovine-eyed drudgery on the consumption-driven machine. I couldn't stand it.

And so I book a one-way flight to Mumbai, packing a toothbrush, a couple of T-shirts, socks and undies, an old-school film camera, a few empty journals, novels and plasters. I throw it all into my dad's old backpack (which is 28 years old by that point), find my "green mamba" South African passport and leave. (Later, everyone will ask me what my parents thought – and, to be honest, I have no idea. I think by this point they knew that when I decided I would do something, nothing could stop me. At DSG, I had put my pocket money into a tiny share portfolio on PSG that I used to manage online – R50 here and there, which had grown into a couple of thousand by the time I finished school. This felt like an absolute fortune for a 17-year-old in 2011 and enough to get a resourceful teenager pretty far in India. My parents had learnt to be laid-back with me, but sometimes their laissez-faire attitude went a bit too far.)

After a couple of months of travelling, I wind up in

Burma and find myself living in a treehouse. One night, the region is struck by an earthquake. Earthquakes are terrifying at the best of times, but when you're lying in a hammock in the dark, in a rickety treehouse in the middle of the jungle, the raw, brutal reality of these beautiful, shell-shocking forces of nature really hits home.

Once the earth's shaking has subsided, I scramble out of the treehouse in the sweltering night and hitch a ride on the back of a moped to the closest village, swatting wildly at mosquitoes along the way. Eventually, we get there and I find a lone landline telephone that offers a crackly connection to the outside world. I call home, expecting panicked, sobbing cries of, "Are you alive? Must we fly you out?" Surely the news of this natural disaster would have reached home by now.

The phone rings for about two whole bloody minutes before a faraway voice answers and says, "Hello?" In the background, I can hear voices and music.

"Mom! It's me! I'm alive! Don't worry. The earthquake has passed – tell Dad I'm okay!" I yell.

There is a long silence from my mother, and then she shouts back, "Huh? Oh – hello?! Hello, darling, dreadful time to chat, very, very busy, must dash! So fab that you're having fun! Anyway, got to run! Tah-tah!" The phone goes dead.

Classic. I buy a Coca-Cola and sit on a dirty white plastic chair next to some sleeping dogs, waiting for the dawn so I can walk back to what is left of my treehouse.

The smelly teenage backpacker that I've become pounds the pavements of the world with worn-out sneakers and a huge smile. I witness the dawn of my 18th birthday sitting cross-legged at the Taj Mahal as it turns from inky blue to pink, red and finally a dazzling white by 5am. I am utterly alone at the temple dedicated to love. I think of the words of Rabindranath Tagore when he said that the Taj Mahal was a "teardrop on the face of eternity".

Somewhere along the way, I exchange my passport for an old Enfield motorbike to see more of India, first heading north to Rajasthan and then on to Rishikesh. If I return the bike in working order, I'll get my passport back.

I then travel halfway around the world and spend weeks trekking and canoeing along the Amazon River, finally arriving on the Inca Trail. I follow it to Machu Picchu and witness the dawn through the Sun Gate. I move among hippies galore who traipse about barefoot and give me little animal skulls and rocks. I carry a scrap of paper with me that a man in India gave me. He had scribbled something on it and wordlessly handed it to me. I still have it. It says, "Ahmen Brahma chakra dai." Back then, I had no idea what it meant, both the words or why he had given it to me, but he told me it was a gift to share.

What I discover on my mad dash around the globe is that the world is vast and life is long when you strip away the bullshit of baggage that you probably didn't even choose to pick up in the first place. The world is much bigger than social media or the news have led me to believe. I encounter more people and have more experiences than I ever dreamed of from my little corner of South Africa. I also discover that I can lose myself and rediscover myself all in a day, and that I can find answers for myself and whatever version of truth the moment calls for.

Sometimes truth speaks to me softly, but at times it roars. Does the world end with a bang or a whimper?

There are millions of alleyways in this world filled with homes and shops and hope and despair. Quiet desperation and soaring ambition. Desire, damnation and unexpected kindness that flutters and lands gently.

Backpacking as an 18-year-old with hardly any money means I am constantly on street level. I have grown up a ferocious reader, so I'm not naive, but the real world, as Gandalf told us, is "out there". The world I've read about in literature and the world that fills my nostrils and pushes back against the soles of my worn sneakers are two very different things. There is no glory in poverty and no glamour in the unknown suffering that I witness from quiet rooms in forgotten corners.

I've gone out to find Life, and while I see unimaginable beauty in our world, I am also confronted with injustice on a massive scale, too loud to shut out and too pervasive to ignore. I see that there are so many desperate and suffering people who need help, who need a voice, who need hope. I see that the being I am – mostly uneducated, hitchhiking and backpacking from temple to jungle to youth hostel – isn't going to help them or right the injustices in the world. I often feel powerless. But along the way, I also realise that I have a responsibility to somehow make "it" better. I am fired up by that knowledge.

Meeting that responsibility becomes one of the defining themes of my life. Using whatever strength I have in my bones and wit in my brain, I decide to return South Africa, get to work, work, work and create a world that feels a little better. I will do something extraordinary.

There's this feeling you get when you enter a new country. There's nowhere to go but everywhere. Hop on a train and go north, or perhaps south? Catch a bus and go east, walk down a path and stay in a hut. Who knows, who cares? Time isn't real. There is no tomorrow, only an infinite present, punctuated only by the occasional need to eat and keep moving your feet. Anywhere, everywhere, maybe following a cute boy or a curious-looking monkey down a bizarre, cobble-stoned street in Kathmandu.

It is also a lonely time. I briefly fall in love for the first time with another 18-year-old backpacker, a Dutch boy I meet on Isla del Sol in Bolivia, but my search for ultimate freedom necessitates a bit of loneliness. People are a tether, and I am on a solo quest. When I'm finally ready for society, to come back to a village or town and share the stories I've gathered on my search for new frontiers, everyone is gone. New town, new faces, new people, no people. I spend many days alone.

It's easy to feel forgotten about. Or that the world is too big. I used to believe it was the purest form of freedom. I don't know if I still believe that. I think I now believe that freedom is a state of mind. I used to stand on train platforms heading out to a new destination or at the top of a mountain after a long, hard and silent upward climb, completely unattached to everything – society, family, career, studies, identity, self. It was pure detachment. And I have never felt more crushed than I did in those moments. More caged in.

It is during this time that I realise that what is driving me so relentlessly isn't a quest for the truth. It feels like

I am running from a trauma I cannot articulate, from words my mouth have never formed, from events I refuse to acknowledge that have grown in the corners of my mind like a seeping disease, rotting slowly, like tentacles of bacteria creeping towards me to suffocate me. So, I run, and run further still, quite literally circumnavigating the globe before I am 19 years old.

Going from Rajasthan to the Far East, I touch down in Beijing. My insomnia-induced midnight walks through Shanghai. The earthquake in Burma in the infamous treehouse and the complete sense of powerlessness. This isn't it. Keep moving. Across the Pacific to sunny California and my first days in Silicon Valley. I am poor and sleep on couches and sing for my supper, trading visions of the future and swapping hostel books for startup books. It's the first time I say the word: "Startup … startup." I roll it around my tongue. It is delightful. It is the first time I meet people who have turned their frustrations with the world into practical solutions. It leaves me breathless. California is also the first time I get stoned with one of my housemates who rolls the most obscenely humongous joints I've ever seen. We walk around Berkeley talking about the future or eating tacos in the sun, completely baked on hilarity and chaotic youth.

California draws me in, but my restlessness is overwhelming. Before I can let myself be happy, I get on a flight to Lima and overland it to Bolivia. I wake up to swampy mornings along the Amazon with sweaty, beautiful and equally lost men whom I love and then hate in quick succession. Every day, I grow more desperate for a sense of belonging.

CHAPTER 10

A NIGHT IN PRISON

After I've been on the road for many months, my last stop before returning to South Africa is La Paz. I don't intend to stay long, but I want to make it to Iguazu Falls on the border with Brazil before my flight out of Buenos Aires. Communicating across language barriers has become second nature to me after months of travelling through so many countries where English is sparse at best. I believe that most humans share the same range of emotions and desires, so communication without actual words is entirely possible by tone of voice, facial expressions, body language and gestures. These methods are enough to help me get by.

On my first evening in La Paz, at around 8pm, I buy a bus ticket for one of those crazy, 10-hour bus rides that traverse the length and breadth of the massive continent of South America – the long-distance-travel modus operandi for many. The bus is leaving at midnight. The heat of the day has passed. The night has grown icy, and I am starting to get cold. I am skinny from months of not being able to afford a solid meal, and my clothes are worn and full of holes and do nothing to keep me warm.

I decide to spend a couple of pesos at a late-night cafe and get a cup of coffee to warm me up. I heave my backpack onto my back and thread my way through the evening crowds to a dimly lit street cafe. There are dodgy characters on the street but, having grown up in South Africa, this is nothing new to me. I like to believe I am streetwise, and my eyes sweep my surroundings to assess any possible risk. The place seems safe enough. I order *un café con leche, por favor* and a little tube of *dulce de leche*, that deliciously sweet South American caramel nectar of the gods, and plonk myself down at a table. I take out *The English Patient*, the book I swapped on Isla del Sol for my previous one, and find the page I'm on. The coffee is strong and bitter, but thankfully it is hot. I eagerly sip it as I follow Count László Almásy flying over the Sahara Desert back to Katharine Clifton, who lies dying in the cave of swimmers...

I look down at my watch: a 1944 Tissot that belonged to my grandfather, Leslie Procter. It is 11.30pm. He was an Englishman, born in Penang and educated at Cambridge, after which he emigrated to the southernmost tip of Africa. The dregs of the coffee lie thick in the bottom of the cup. I heave my backpack onto my back again and make for the door. Outside, I feel a strange liquid hit me out of nowhere, milky white and pungent. Sour milk. I stop and look down. It is disgusting, but I'm not devastated because my clothes are all old and worn anyway. Either way, I have a bus to catch and a border to cross. Suddenly, a shortish man with an open face and wearing glasses approaches me and says in a heavily accented voice: "Oh my God, I am so sorry! These kids play this game with tourists where they try to throw things at them … I am so sorry! Here, let me help you, I have tissues."

He hands me a box of tissues. Not suspecting a thing, I wipe myself down, grateful for his kindness. "*Gracias, señor*! But I have to catch my bus!"

"No, *señorita*, let me help you quickly, especially if you have a long trip – here, take your bag off and I'll get the worst of it off your back!"

I lower my bag slowly and cautiously, but before it is even unhooked from my arms, two men appear. In one swift movement, they grab my bag and sprint off into the midnight alleyways. For a moment I can say nothing. I am numb with shock. A heartbeat later, I shout, "Motherfuckers!" and sprint off after them. I don't care for the dirty clothes or even the handful of pesos or my old cellphone in there – my travel insurance will cover that. What I care about is my camera's SD card with all my gazillions of photos and my diary that I have kept daily for the past 12 months. I round the corner. I see them run and then … nothing. They have disappeared into thin air. I spin around and try to ask the people next to me, "*Los viste?*" Blank stares. "*Los viste? Me robaron el bolso!*"

They stare ahead. Disinterested. Panic rising, I dart through the crowd, looking for the discarded journal. Nothing. Of course, the "nice" man is nowhere to be seen. Then my heart stops and my blood turns to ice – fuck! My fucking passport! I clutch at my chest, suddenly remembering the little pouch I bought that very morning from a Quechua woman in the village I had stayed in the night before. I never buy clutter and trinkets, but she told me that I'd soon need it, so I spent the 10 pesos. And there, dangling against my heart, is the little woven sack with my green South African passport stuffed inside. I'd thought to put it there just for the hell of it. It is now my sole possession. (To this day I still keep my passport in it.)

I sit down on the curb, at a loss for what to do next. I have no money and no idea where to go. It is probably close to 1am by now, and the street is all but empty except for a lingering group of men. There is a dark feeling. I pick up a malicious energy in the icy air. I walk along the main road, sticking to the best-lit areas, until at last I find a police station. In broken Spanish, I explain that I have no money after being robbed. They say they would normally take me to a hotel where I could call the South African embassy in Peru to assist me, but all the hotels are closed. The only place for me to spend the night is in one of their empty cells. And so I spend the next few freezing hours in a dark, dank prison cell in downtown La Paz, feeling – I'm not going to lie – pretty majorly put out. It's hardly the Ritz Carlton. As the sun rises, I make my way to a hotel and decide that my best bet is to call the person I know will always be my safe harbour, who will always come to my rescue and have my back. I call my dad.

"Dr Procter speaking."

"Dad, it's me. I'm in Bolivia. Look – I'm fine, I'm not hurt, but all my stuff has been stolen. There's no rush to cancel my cards because there's no money in the accounts, but it's probably worth cancelling them anyway."

"Are you sure you're okay? Are you hurt? Did anyone hurt you or touch you?!"

"No, no, I'm fine. Just a bit miserable and hungry, but I'll walk it off."

Once he knows that I am unharmed, the rage begins. "I told you this was a bad idea! I told you this would happen … you are so impulsive! When are you going to start thinking about the consequences of your flippant behaviour? You're getting on the next flight to leave that godforsaken country, and you're enrolling at university – I've had enough of this gallivanting."

"Honestly, I'm fine! And I have a flight leaving Buenos Aires anyway in seven days! No point wasting the money buying a new ticket. I'll survive another week, catch my original flight and see you in a bit, okay?"

"How are you going to survive until then?"

"Um, well. Could you spot me some cash? I'll pay you back, promise!"

"I thought you had no money in your account?"

"I'll pay you back for everything one day, Dad, for real. All of it. And then some. Just wire some cash to my hotel, please." I have the hotel's name and bank details. "I'll see you in a week! Try not to stress too much, it makes you age faster, ha ha. Alright, see you soon. Bye."

Seven days to kill. If I were a reasonable person, I would head straight to Buenos Aires, check into a simple, clean hotel and stay away from adventure until I get home. But that's not my style. If I were the kind of girl who played it safe, you wouldn't be reading this book, would you?

A coffee, a *dulce de leche* (my entire diet for all those weeks – it's a bloody miracle I didn't get scurvy) and a couple of hours later, I am back at the bus station with a one-way ticket for the border of Brazil. I am sticking to my plan to see the Iguazu Falls with the last of my cash. From there, I will hitch my way down half a continent to Buenos Aires and sleep for three nights on the couch of a medical student I have arranged to meet in Paseo El Rosedal Garden – before hopefully borrowing two pesos to catch the bus to the airport.

So, in September 2011, I find myself on a computer in the common room of a youth hostel in Buenos Aires. Having lost almost all my stuff to those "sour-milk thieves" in La Paz, I am now travelling super-light.

I google "University of Cape Town" and up pops UCT's website. I click on "Apply".

At the age of 15, I discovered Descartes and the idea of doubting everything beyond "I think, therefore I am". The dropdown menu of the website shows "Faculty of Science", and another judicious click takes me to the Physics page. I then go on to FlySAA, the South African Airways website, and check in for my flight back to South Africa. It is time to go home.

The following day, not exactly looking like Miss Universe in my holey clothes without a purse or a peso, I board my SAA flight and begin my transatlantic trip to Johannesburg, the City of Gold. A few hours later, I am on a connecting flight to Cape Town, the Mother City.

CHAPTER 11

MY INGLORIOUS FAILURE

I begin studying for my science degree in physics at UCT in 2012 and quickly become aware of the politics and power structures on campus. At the ripe old age of 18, I've come to regard politics as exhausting. Plus, I've never really been one for groups because most of my life I have felt like an outsider. So while I am not interested in becoming involved in politics per se, I am also simply far too opinionated and hard-headed *not* to get involved if decisions are being made that I disagree with. I hear about the Student Representative Council (SRC) elections the day before applications are due to close and decide on a whim to enter the race.

I stay up until dawn putting my application together. Just as the sun peeks over the Hottentots Holland mountains, I arrive on campus to submit my application at the Steve Biko Students' Union building.

Dawn can be spectacular on UCT's Upper Campus. On this early morning, there are a handful of students who have just arrived back from a night out. They are sitting on

Jammie Steps watching the sun rise over the expanse of the southern suburbs and the Cape Flats. Some are finishing off beers, some eating pizza. With smudged makeup and arms around shoulders, they are young and glorious, with their entire future ahead of them although they probably have no idea what responsibility even smells like. Their connection to each other exudes beauty, but I don't pause as I pass them. I'm on a mission, scaling the stairs to the Students' Union building. The deadline for my submission is imminent.

Once the submissions are in, the campaigning begins. I have absolutely no idea of what I'm in for. Most of the student political parties have heavy subsidies and support from the parent political organisations – parties that are all desperate to recruit the next generation of voters by winning on campuses. I have entered as an independent candidate. I have no political affiliation, allies or campaigning agenda other than some crazy posters I hastily designed the night before on Microsoft PowerPoint. They feature me on a toy motorbike. (To this day, I have no idea why I did that. It just seemed hilarious at the time.)

I put every inch of myself into my campaign. I stage flash mobs in the food court and make my crazy campaign posters the background image on every lecture-theatre computer. While the other candidates have been practising their speeches for weeks, if not months, with the guidance of senior party officials across the political spectrum, I only have pure chutzpah to guide me. The one thing I'm certain of is that I must stand out. So, Step One is to separate myself from the rest of the candidates. The day before campaigning began, I bought a bright red trench coat, sewed my candidate number onto the back and donned a massive blue wig. I walked to campus and into a lecture theatre for the first set of campaigning speeches with blue hair and dressed head to foot in red.

I can't stand prepared speeches. I find them inauthentic and limp, and when they are overrehearsed, they often reek of duplicity. I prefer to just stand up in front of the audience, shoot from the hip and speak my truth. In my campaign speeches, I say who I am, why I'm running and what I intend to do. I want to be real and relevant and straightforward, so I put my heart and soul into those speeches. It feels like I truly connect with people. Whenever I speak, there is usually silence in the room. The audience appears to be focused on me, with no one's head bowed to look at their cellphones. I am convinced they are hanging on my every word.

While the other candidates stare above the heads of the crowd and repeat their rehearsed lines – often party dogma – to drive home the same message over and over again, treating the audience as if they're children, I try to appeal to people on a deeper level. I question the very nature of power structures and progress. I feel an authentic connection between myself and the electorate at the university.

But oh boy, am I in for a surprise – because it turns out that I was dead wrong. When the results come out two weeks later, I have hardly made a mark. I am number 18 on the list. The top 17 candidates get into office. So much for an authentic human connection. I'm shocked. I really thought I had nailed it, but I clearly missed the boat. After all that effort, I have failed.

I'm a bad loser. After the results come out, I feel deep shame burning through my veins. I have humiliated myself. I am an abject public failure.

I gather all my campaign material – the posters, the stickers, even the blue wig and red clothes – and go down to the parking lot outside the block of flats where I live. I build a bonfire and burn everything. If I'd won, I would be in the SRC offices right now, negotiating the various positions along with the other electees, vying for the presidency and establishing a 100-day plan to start with an unforgettable bang. Instead, I have lost, ingloriously.

A couple of my friends kept texting me, wanting to come over to my place to be with me, to take me out somewhere to have fun. But I sulk like a brat and not only turn my phone off but also smash it like a toddler throwing a tantrum. I feel so alone. All through my campaign I have isolated myself, but now I am too petty and vain to accept support. I stand in the parking lot, watching the plastic wig sizzle and melt in the fire.

Failure might look bad, but cowardice looks way worse. I can't face going back to university. I can't face myself, let alone anyone else. The pity, the derision, the fall from grace, all those dreams and plans and goals – all gone.

Later, this experience will stand me in good stead when it comes to my future failings. Along the way, I've learnt that sometimes you try really hard but all you get is egg on your face. It can often feel like a world of noes and doors slammed in your face.

There's a wonderful quote by Churchill that says success is about going from failure to failure without losing your enthusiasm. After losing the SRC election, I've certainly lost my drive and my sense of humour. I stand alone on that tragic afternoon, watching the flames in the parking lot erase my election material.

Over the next few years, I will come to understand that learning how to fail well is one of the greatest lessons in life. It's a gift to take stock, reassess and learn how to be better and win the next time. It's simply market feedback. It's the world telling you what works and what doesn't. It's learning the rules of the game in real time. There's honour in defeat if it's done authentically. It can be an opportunity to face yourself and learn humility. But back then, I'm still so consumed by my bruised ego and the torturous feelings of disgrace that all I can do is run. So, I decide to take refuge in the place where I have always regained myself: the mountains and my solitude.

CHAPTER 12

LICKING MY WOUNDS ON KILIMANJARO

Me being me, I can't simply go for a trot up Lion's Head or saunter up Table Mountain. So, I go online and book a flight to Moshi, a little town right at the foot of Mount Kilimanjaro in the north of Tanzania.

I arrive a few days later. I am unfit and morally defeated. I feel that the only way I can come back from my fall is to summit this mountain. Kilimanjaro is the highest point on the African continent, standing like a giant at just under 6 000 metres tall. Tanzania is a beautiful country, and as soon as I arrive in the town, I begin to acclimatise. I didn't tell anyone I was leaving. I didn't believe anyone would even notice that I was gone.

In the town, I gather the necessary gear, going with what the shop assistant suggests in his broken English: boots, thermal underwear, a couple of shirts and hiking poles. "That should do it, right?"

"*Ndio, ndio, ni sawa!*"

It sounds good to me. The next day, I join a trekking group and we start our ascent.

The first day is straightforward. I am still sulking and feeling sorry for myself, so I don't engage with the group (mostly German and American tourists) whose cheerfulness pisses me off no end. For God's sake, can they stop looking so happy?! I keep to myself at the front, trying to beat everyone to prove in some petty way that I can still win at something.

On the second day, I decide to join the guides for breakfast instead of eating with the tourists. I walk to the clump of trees where they are sitting, and they hand me a bowl of a spicy, curry-type dish. I love spicy food. My mood picks up and I feel more upbeat, sitting in the equatorial heat in my hiking gear, listening to the guides chatting and laughing. For the first time in days, I manage to escape my head. It feels like I have been given a broader perspective. I am reminded again of how big the world is, and I have a tiny glimpse into the possibility of moving on from the failure that seemed so all-encompassing. Perhaps there is the possibility of a second chance? Maybe I can try again?

Fate has another plan for me. We begin our trek after breakfast. About an hour later, the first twitch of bodily discontent hits. I keep going, trying to force myself to allow it to pass. I always say, "I don't get sick." No matter how bad things might feel, I keep repeating this to myself and anyone else for that matter – that I simply do not get sick. "Weakness of mind is weakness of body," I have always told myself. Mindset is everything. "I do not get sick." Two hours later, I am retching up everything in my body. I'm weak and dizzy and begin shaking all over.

The usual suspect on the mountain at this high altitude is AMS – acute mountain sickness. This happens when the haemoglobin in your blood fails to adjust to carry enough oxygen to your essential organs, depleting your body of oxygen. It can often be fatal. Usually, if you get AMS, you turn around or you die.

By the next morning, I am in a sorry state. Everyone is telling me to turn around. We have already seen the emergency medical helicopter making frequent trips up and down the mountain, carting to hospital various dying hikers who pushed themselves beyond their limits. Everyone thinks I will be next.

One of the German hikers in our group has a finger oximeter. It's a little device that you put on your forefinger to measure oxygen levels in your bloodstream. (They will become quite popular after the onset of Covid-19.) That night, I borrow his oximeter and see that my blood oxygen is 90%, which is excellent for our altitude of 4 000 metres.

My guess is that I don't have AMS but rather some sort of food poisoning from the somewhat unfamiliar breakfast I ate with the guides. The other telltale sign is that I don't have a headache, only intense stomach cramps, and AMS almost always presents with a headache from insufficient oxygen reaching the brain. I tell the guides and the rest of the hiking party that I will not turn back. The group is incredulous. No one wants a dead hiker on their hands, which will surely be a total mood killer and probably ruin all the photos. But I am adamant. The guide hands me an indemnity document, stating that I refused the recommendation to turn around and that my life is in my own hands. I sign it and continue trekking.

The pain is unbelievable. I've experienced food poisoning before – that twisting in your gut, like some beefy-armed washerwoman is simultaneously wringing your stomach and intestines out to dry. It's ghastly. Now, imagine that, except you're also at 4 000 metres above sea level and climbing rapidly. I can't eat anything without the pain intensifying. If I try, I puke it straight up again. I grow weaker until my leg muscles scream in protest with every step. There is nothing, no carbs or sugars or proteins, for my body to burn to carry me forward.

As I ascend, I take two or three steps, then hunch over and clutch at my guts, which twist inside me. With every step, the oxygen in my airways diminishes. My breath is rasping, which is helluva unnerving for everyone in the group. At night, I huddle in a ball in the tent next to my tent mate, too weak to change out of my hiking clothes and shivering and shaking from pain and exhaustion.

"No matter," I tell myself. "You will summit or you will die. There is no alternative. There is no other way."

Something deep is driving me. I just have to get through this and to the top, then I can turn around and go home. Or die somewhere up on that peak. Some madness has overtaken me. My entire world has been reduced to this mountain, to these raw, jagged rocks, the massive blue sky, the cold, clear and biting air, my boots and blisters, my pain and my delusions. I now exist without a past, without needing a future. I just have to get to the top.

CHAPTER 13

DO OR DIE

Finally, summit night arrives. I've been awake for hours already, shivering with occasional spasms in my gut, as the minutes tick by. I keep glancing at my watch, waiting for any sound or movement in the camp to signal that we are ready. The plan is to leave at midnight to summit as dawn rolls in. It would be easy to turn back, to just give up. No one would care. In fact, they would prefer it. No one back home would know because no one there is even aware that I have come here.

Just give up. The pain will go. Just give up. Imagine how much better you'd feel. This running narrative whirs through my brain. I know I can't argue with it or outwit it. I have absolutely no energy left.

The hours leading up to the summit bid are excruciating. But the anticipation of pain is often so much worse than the pain itself. Seneca once said, "There are more things likely to frighten us than to crush us; we suffer more often in imagination than in reality." As the minutes drag by, I lie in the tent and try to get as much oxygen into my blood as possible while massaging my gut. Sleep is impossible.

In that dark, freezing and airless night on the slopes of Kilimanjaro, I wait alone, pain occasionally searing my intestines and my legs aching and weak. Those hours feel like being on the edge of a razor blade slowly slicing into my skin along every nerve edge. But I sit through it and somehow manage to control my mind and quell my fear.

Finally, I decide that it is time.

There is an urgency to get going, with a window in the weather before conditions turn impossible again. In my crazy desire to summit, I decide to leave an hour before the others because of my slow pace. I boot up and crawl out of the tent. It is pitch dark out on the mountain. Everyone is still sleeping. I stand for a moment, feeling the strange freedom of anonymity that comes with being in the dark. There are also shades of terror from a lifetime of fearing the dark. (I slept with a light on in my bathroom right into my mid-twenties.)

I switch on my headlamp and turn towards the path up Kilimanjaro. A silent Swahili guide walks behind me.

It is far worse than I imagined. Almost immediately, I start vomiting again. There is no food in me – there hasn't been any in days – so all that is left is bile. The taste in my mouth is foul, no matter how much I try to rinse with the icy water.

It is freezing cold and the cheap, shoddy gear I bought in town is no match for the elevation. If I stop moving for too long, my body will grow numb from the cold and stop responding. I am literally freezing. When I inch forward, my gut twists and I retch and heave and cough as I struggle to breathe. I tell myself that it won't last forever and that I will be at the top before I know it. I look down at my grandfather's Tissot watch. It is 1am. Okay, sunrise is at 6am. When the sun rises, I tell myself, I will be warm, then I can rest. It will be fine. Just get to 6am, I tell myself. One more step. Check the time: 1.03am. Oh, God. Another step.

Slowly, at a snail's pace, I inch my way up. One more step. 1.09am. By now, the other hikers have begun their summit bid and are moving fast. They soon overtake me, which is rather discouraging if you're the kind of person (like me) who bases your self-worth on always winning. I push the thought of the other hikers out of my mind and go back to thinking about the next step I have to take. Foot up, forward, down. Breathe. 1.12am.

I trek and trek through the dark, icy night. Surely I have to be close to the top by now? I look up, and as far as I can see there is a line of headlamps stretching up above me. I still have miles to go. The thought suddenly defeats me. I sit down and begin to cry, the tears freezing on my face. "I can't do it, I can't do it," I sob to myself. "I can't do it, I'm not strong enough." But they are just words, because deep down, I already know that I will do it. *You will summit or you will die. There is no alternative.* I know I can't look up or at the time again, because thinking about the future isn't helping. Somehow, I have to get up and take another step. Then another. And another. And if it is my karma to die trying, then so be it.

I heave myself to my feet. Hunched over and gasping, I take that next step. And then another, and another. "One more step" becomes my mantra. Time takes on a different quality after that – and to this day it's never quite gone back to what it was before. It's as if all my life I have been living outside my body, watching my life go by as a spectator, vaguely aware of the world that exists but where, up to now, I've just been going through the motions.

Even in India, Peru and Burma, I'd physically been there but it had somehow felt like it was all happening around me, to someone else, to a clone of Alexandria. It was as if this life was a test run and the real one was only coming round later. I kept asking myself: where is Life? Where is it? When will I feel complete, real and alive? But these questions were never answered.

Until now, I have existed in a haze of distractions: social mind games and manoeuvres, social media and status signalling, a "fit in or fuck off" education, mindless family tasks, inherited ideas around identity, feeling like I am in the sausage factory of the future that will make me a tax-paying, law-abiding citizen of consumerism, pumping the machine of economic growth for some banker on Wall Street to gamble with.

At 3am on the side of the mountain at 5 400 metres, racked with pain and with no escape, I am hyper-aware that this is it. *This is real.* It all becomes clear: this world, this life, the choices I made, the fact that I am here, and I'm alive and I have been granted the opportunity to *do* something worthwhile.

I decide that if I make it down the mountain, if I survive, I will face the failure I ran away from, and that I will never again see failure as the end of the road but rather as an opportunity to come up with something even better. Now that I am experiencing reality coupled with excruciating pain, it is clear to me that almost anything else life throws at me will be bearable.

In that moment of extreme perspective, I see the difference between security and freedom, between truth and hollow words, between self-pity and grace, between living in a state of committed action and succumbing to lies, laziness and comfort. On that freezing mountain, I am completely naked. There is nothing to hide behind.

Just before the sun rises, the guide begins to sing in Swahili. He has kept pace with me all night, and now his song is setting the pace for my steps, my physical mantra. Clearly and softly his voice fills the silent night mountain air that envelops us. *One more step.* The light in the sky begins changing colour. I can see the first hints of the darkness lifting.

"We are almost at the plateau," he tells me.

One more step.

One more step.

The snow is ankle-deep. It crunches under our boots. My fingers are completely numb. There is vomit frozen around my face and on my clothes. No matter. I feel at peace, having reached an understanding with the pain in every inch of my legs, gut, head, hands and feet. I no longer fear it. I simply let it be.

There is an ocean that separates pain and suffering.

One more step. Above me, the stars shine in their billions, a terrifying number of stars, not necessitating any explanation.

Eventually, the sky turns glorious pink. We switch off our headlamps. From my hunched-up, semi-crawling position, I stop clutching at my stomach, stretch up and turn around to face the great plains of the Serengeti that extend from Kilimanjaro, the largest free-standing mountain in the world. I can see the slight curvature of our home planet, hanging suspended in the cosmos. And I see that the Earth is pure and huge and fresh and brave and clean and true on yet another morning of existence; that I get to experience a new dawn of life.

The night has passed, like it always does. *This too shall pass*. And so it has.

We have reached the plateau. As I stare at the miraculous beauty, I sob. I stand in blank, wordless amazement, the tears frozen on my cheeks. The sunlight touches the exposed parts of my skin. I can feel each particle, each photon of light, entering my frozen pores and warming the blood that runs through my veins and capillaries. It feels as though the atoms that make me will burst apart, that my entire life's meaning is contained in those rays. I'm not a religious person, but there on the plateau, I understand that this sunrise on Kilimanjaro is grace.

I have reached the summit. I am 20 years old.

Two days later, we are back in Moshi. I turn my cell phone on for the first time in over a week. I have a bunch of messages, missed calls and notifications. There are the usual ones from friends and family asking where the hell I am, but there is one that I wasn't expecting. Keenan, the secretary-general of the SRC, says he needs to get hold of me urgently. I tell him I'll be back in Cape Town in two days' time, and we schedule a meeting at a coffee shop in Newlands – one that serves a mind-blowingly good cheesecake that I feel I desperately deserve.

Three days later, I make my way to the meeting. Before

he even opens his mouth, I start speaking. "Look, Keenan, I'm sorry I didn't say this to you sooner, but massive congrats for making it onto the SRC for a second term. You're amazing, and you deserve this. I'm sorry I didn't say it to you on the day, but I guess I had some growing up to do."

He laughs, brushes it aside in his usual diplomatic fashion and orders two slices of cheesecake. Now he gets down to business. One of the candidates who made it onto the SRC has been asked to leave because of a serious misdemeanour, and since I'm next on the list, I am up for the post, should the Student Assembly ratify my selection.

A week later, after I have addressed the Student Assembly and the rest of the SRC, my selection is approved and I am sworn in.

Here's the funny thing about life. When I originally campaigned for student governance, with my crazy blue hair, red garb, flash mobs and grand speeches, I was running for the presidency. In my usual egotistical manner, I would settle for nothing less than the top job.

When I eventually join the SRC a few weeks after my failed campaign, I'm asked to fill the position of day students' coordinator to help students who are living out of res and off campus. (In retrospect, I'm sure they gave me that position because nobody else wanted it.) The student-digs situation is an absolute shitshow. But this is when I first have the idea of creating a student housing website where my friends and peers can find safe and affordable accommodation. This leads me to DigsConnect.

CHAPTER 14

#FEESMUSTFALL & THE STUDENT HOUSING CRISIS

In early 2016, I arrive on campus on the first day of the new semester to find a group of students sitting in the middle of Residence Road, holding signs that read "Student housing crisis at UCT" and "Shackville". Atop a flight of stone stairs, behind the empty plinth where the statue of Cecil John Rhodes once stood, is an corrugated-iron shack. Graffitied on its wall is a slogan: "This is the State of our Nation".

This area will soon become ground zero for demonstrations that will spread like wildfire and expose the student housing crisis across South Africa's 26 public universities and various colleges. Shackville draws the attention of the mass media and students across the country. The subsequent destruction and removal of the shack and the arrests of its occupants throw petrol on the fire. It certainly captures my attention.

In the rhetoric of post-apartheid South Africa, which

positions education as the vehicle to lift people out of poverty, why is the symbol of student accommodation a shack? While some of these students have government funding to pay for their accommodation, the system is so badly mismanaged that they either get scammed or never receive what they have been promised. Thousands of students arrive on campus for another academic year, only to end up homeless.

The idea that tech and our phones can open a portal to better services than we currently had is exemplified by the launch of Uber on campus, with privileged students enthralled by the idea of hailing a cab from their phones. It has also recently become possible to start paying for things with our phones by scanning QR codes at the campus cafés to buy a sandwich or chicken noodles for lunch. All around us, new ways of accessing better services are taking off. However, when it comes to housing, many students cannot find basic accommodation and often resort to sleeping in lecture theatres or the library. The rooms are there; they are just impossible to find. If you do find accommodation, it is usually via a faded piece of A4 paper pinned to the notice board outside the library, or through a fortuitous conversation with the guy next to you in organic chemistry class who knows someone who is moving out of their digs. But if you don't know anyone or get to the notice board in time, you are screwed. Tragically, for these students, the great promise of education is a joke. I have no idea during the early days of Shackville just how deep and dire the problem is, until I take up my SRC position as day students' coordinator.

On my first day as an SRC member, I wheel my bicycle out the front door of our digs and cycle down Rondebosch Main Road on my way to Upper Campus. UCT is halfway up Table Mountain, so it's a hell of a ride. By the time I arrive at the bicycle rack, I'm sweating. I then head up Jammie Steps towards the library, turn right and then left, up the stairs and into the Steve Biko building. The SRC is housed on the seventh floor and, as is my habit, I take the stairs two at a time, driven by impatience and the sense of urgency that has lined my epidermis and filled my veins since I can remember. It's a go-go-go feeling that makes me walk at twice the pace of everyone else, rush upstairs, accumulate thousands of rand in speeding fines as I hurtle through traffic, and run around slow pedestrians like a seasoned expert. I don't do it to be antisocial; I just need things to move, you know. I just need a bit of pace.

On that first morning, the door to the SRC offices is standing wide open. A woman, Zwelile, is sitting at the front desk. I soon discover my office is in room 7.

The corridor is lined with photos of previous SRC members. My photo is already on my front door. It feels like a big deal. Inside, the windows have been flung wide open, with a view of the campuses and the southern suburbs of Cape Town, all the way to the Hottentots Holland mountain range.

The extent of the student housing crisis soon becomes apparent to me. Meeting requests flood in from students desperate to find a home. Some are sleeping on friends' couches or paying exorbitant prices at short-term B&Bs,

but the most heartbreaking cases are quite literally homeless, sleeping in lecture theatres or in the 24-hour section of the library.

It is horrifying. UCT has 30 000 enrolled students but only 5 000 beds in residence. There simply is no plan B. This is the same story for students across the country, with zero to at most 50% of students housed on campus. The average rate is below 20%.

At UCT, if students aren't in res, they are sent to a tiny office with one desk where a queue snakes around the building. Inside, they are given a piece of paper with a list of phone numbers and names and told that these are the private accommodation options. It's a total mess. And don't even get me started on the so-called "NSFAS-accredited" process, which is mired in corruption and bribery and on the brink of collapse. (A couple of years later, the National Student Financial Aid Scheme, or NSFAS, will open tender submissions for a student housing platform – my chance to fix the system from the ground up. But more on that later.)

Many of these desperate learners end up queueing outside my little SRC office, pleading for help to find them somewhere to stay. They come from every corner of our diverse country, from Sandton to rural KwaZulu-Natal. Students who flew to Cape Town and students who took 18-hour trips on buses as the first in their families – sometimes even in their towns and villages – to attend university. These young people arrive on campus carrying their belongings, blankets, books and clothes, and the weight of expectations and hopes for a better future for their communities back home. They come to break the cycle of poverty that has robbed so many South Africans of their dignity and left them on their knees with nothing but the bitter taste of empty promises from slimy politicians. And, far too often, these students are left homeless. Most of them wind up in my office, and it is my mandate to fix the system.

As the violent student protests over housing and fees spread through the city and country, with campuses across South Africa joining in, I feel that the need for a solution is beyond urgent. In the context of our country, the student housing crisis is hardly surprising. Many of these universities were built before 1994. When democracy was won, enrolment grew exponentially but the supporting infrastructure at academic institutions didn't keep up. Plenty of South Africa's universities originally accepted white students only. White South Africans account for about 10% of the South African population.

The incompetence of the government and a lack of support from the public sector also mean that students often don't even know if they have been accepted to university or given a residence room until a week or two before classes start. Sometimes, they only find out a week or two *after* classes have started.

Many feel that rectifying the situation is the unenviable duty of the government and the universities – and, to a certain extent, this is true. However, where the government has failed, the private sector is stepping up to the plate.

Landlords call me to say they have spare rooms, vacancies and beds to fill, and they want to know how to advertise these rooms to the students. Ordinary South Africans have realised there is a need in the market, and their natural entrepreneurial spirit has kicked in. It is obvious: what is needed is a website that lists accommodation options for students.

When I finally put two and two together in 2018, after I've left UCT and come up with the idea for DigsConnect, it isn't like I'm trying to be Mark Zuckerberg. There is no Hans Zimmer soundtrack playing in the background. It's just me, with one semester of computer science classes, chucking together a shitty little website over a weekend.

These days, I use phrases like "online marketplace", "buyer" and "seller", or even terms like "ebitda" (earnings before interest, taxes, depreciation and amortisation), when I'm trying to impress an investor. Back then, it's just, you know, obvious.

Of course, it takes me a while between having the idea and actually building that crappy little version 1 of DigsConnect, because in those early days, I suppose I am waiting for "permission". I don't believe I can actually just *do something*. Like, make something that people will use.

(As I sit and write these words in 2023, on my second screen is the back end of DigsConnect. I'm watching as thousands of transactions and interactions and conversations and payments are firing off between our users, and it blows my mind that all these people are finding their *homes* on this thing that I once imagined. That landlords are building their businesses and earning their livelihoods. That in the past few weeks alone, we have generated R50 million in lease value, and that in the next 24 months, R1 billion in leases will be transacted on DigsConnect. Dude. What!)

Back in 2016, I pitch my apparently harebrained idea

excitedly to anyone and everyone who will listen: the protesters, the university administration and the SRC. I argue that if we work together on a solution, we can get it right, fast. I am unfortunately extremely naive and idealistic and probably come across as hyperactive and unfocused. (Which, in all fairness, I 100% was.)

No one seems to pay any attention to what I believe is an obvious solution. Tensions, political point-scoring and red tape are not about to yield to something even closely resembling a solution. Good ideas are simple, but making them work requires a lot of complexity, nuance, commitment and tight coordination. In the heat of the student protests, there are too many emotions, too many big personalities, too much ego, too much talking for magic to happen. Large, angry groups highlight something critical – that society needs change. But big groups are usually too clunky to effect that change.

Amid all the noise and anger, I notice that when the students are waiting their turn to speak to me at the SRC offices, they are always on their phones. The solution is so damn clear to me: they're on their phones already, so they should be able to see all their housing options right there instead of having to wait to chat to me. The name "DigsConnect" comes to me almost instantly because, again, it just sounds so, well … obvious.

CHAPTER 15

BLACK HOLE

My final year of studies for my Bachelor of Science degree is brutal. The housing crisis on campus has left me feeling deeply discouraged and powerless. I battle a dark depression towards the end of 2016 that I simply cannot shake. It feels like I am swimming in deep waters, unable to come up for air. Despite trying my usual tricks of avoidance – like two months backpacking in Italy in the summer, or obsessively going for long, intense runs on the mountain – nothing seems to work. I sink further and further into a deep, dark hole.

My only refuge is the expansive nature around Cape Town. I spend hours each day walking the paths of Table Mountain, exploring the cliffs, swimming in the freezing water of the kelp forests and crying, always crying with an increasing sense of hopelessness as the days grind on. I am 23 years old. I have no idea where I'm going. I have no idea what I'm doing. I am barely passing my course work. I am scraping low 50s only because I somehow smooth-talk my way through the exams with barely articulate arguments.

My scant knowledge is garnered from attending the odd lecture on the days I can get out of bed long enough to make it to campus.

If I do somehow pass, I will graduate with a science degree along with a mishmash of subjects I picked up along the way because they sparked my curiosity: computer science, thermodynamics, English literature, human evolution, archaeology, and history of economics. What the hell will I do with those?

Matriculating from DSG, I'd been so certain that if I just got out of Grahamstown and moved to a cosmopolitan city like Cape Town, I would make it and become everything I had dreamed I was capable of being. But Cape Town is chewing me up and will spit me out. I consider dropping out almost daily. In a mad rush, I apply for odd jobs: "Film producer's assistant, Cape Town, includes travel to California" or "Skipper aboard a Save the Whales Greenpeace ship off to the Arctic Circle". I consider a master's programme in consulting at the London School of Economics and Political Science. I even apply for "Wildlife presenter, Masai Mara". Through all of this, my father somehow talks me off the cliff and I retreat to campus, trying to make sense of the words on the pages of a textbook in front of me but not understanding why the walls are closing in on me. It all just feels so dark.

Somehow, I graduate in 2016. After my final exam, a friend from class, Claire, invites me for tacos at a Mexican restaurant in Woodstock. As we drink iced margaritas and munch on cheesy tortillas, she says, "Proc, enough. You need to see someone. Here's a number. Her name is Kate, and she's different. She gets it. Just call her."

She sends me the number. After we finish our meal, Claire stands up and announces, "A bunch of us are going to a party this evening on Clifton 2nd Beach. See you there?"

"Sure, let's see how it goes and hopefully I make it." I know I will soon be lying on my apartment floor, staring up at the ceiling and watching the light fade from the room as the evening ends and the night sets in. I'll watch the white ceiling turn dark and hate every second, every moment of my life, knowing that nothing I do or say and nowhere I go will make it better. Alone is preferable. When I'm on my own, I can allow myself to be consumed by the sadness without needing to hide it.

Claire leaves me sitting at the table staring at nothing. While I know I have probably passed my final exams, even if dismally, I feel crushing hopelessness. I have underperformed spectacularly at university. There is no feeling quite like unfulfilled potential. Everyone expected me to fail at life, and here I am, fulfilling their premonition. I'm going nowhere. A cockroach lazily makes its way along the floor and saunters out the front door and onto the hot tar outside.

I stand up, push in my chair and make my way out of the grimy Mexican restaurant to the equally grimy streets of Woodstock. For a moment, I just stand there. I can't bear the thought of going home alone. I know the darkness will envelop me there. What is my next step? Where will I go? What should I do? I am shit at everything. Tears prick the corners of my eyes, and self-hatred swells in my chest. *So fucking useless, so fucking useless.* Despite every opportunity given to me, I am a waste of space. Almost mechanically, I take my phone out of my bag and dial. It rings and rings and rings. No answer. Finally, a voicemail box: "Hey, this is Kate. Leave a message and I'll get back to you!"

Yeah, right … The phone beeps.

"Oh, um, hi. It's Alexandria. Claire gave me your number. I, um … urgh … don't worry, wrong number." I hang up. Whatever.

As I get into my car, my phone rings. "Hi, it's Kate. Sorry I missed your call. How are you doing?"

"Oh, um. I dunno, fine. You?"

"Hmm. You don't sound great. Would you like to come in for a chat?"

"Um. I don't know. When?"

"How about right now?"

"I'm actually really busy right now, you know, but like I'll think about it, okay?"

"No, I think you should come in now. Really. My office is on Kloof Street. When can you get here?"

Jesus, this woman is insistent. I feel a flare of irritation. How dare she interrupt my self-pity? How dare she try to solve my problems? They are my problems! But I don't even have the strength to argue. I will go to the stupid appointment and then never see her again.

"Okay, fine, I can be there in 20 minutes."

"I'll be waiting for you, Alexandria. See you now."

Half an hour later, I am sitting across from Kate. Her consulting room is white and beige, with a duck-egg-blue sofa, plants everywhere and a huge window that looks out over the mountain. It smells of incense.

From the moment I enter her space, Kate's serenity collides with my self-loathing and darkness. We pause for a moment to acknowledge the energy exchange as I sit down cross-legged on the couch.

"So, you're a bit of a mess," she says.

"Well, life is a bloody joke, isn't it?" I answer curtly.

"Is it?"

"Obviously. Are you kidding me? What kind of a stupid question is that? Surely you know how much suffering there is in the world? The injustice?! The hunger?! The entire system is rigged. There is poverty literally wherever I look. On this street, I can see beggars everywhere without any hope, without anyone fighting for them. Surely you know that humans are destroying the planet, that climate change is destroying habitats, killing millions of species … there's water insecurity, and it's only increasing! I mean, are you ignorant?! Do you know how many refugees there are in the world? Do you know how many people are suffering from HIV and Aids?! Are you even faintly aware of how corrupt all governments are?! Well, are you?!"

I am furious. Tears of rage pour down my cheeks. My throat feels tight and my voice is thick. I hate how weak I sound, how pathetic I am.

"We're on a bloody rock in a void. Everyone is going to die, so what's the bloody point? What's the point of all this suffering? Why be born only to feel shit and die? What the actual fuck kind of cruelty is that? All I feel is disgust for whatever it was that made this happen! I can't stand it. I can't stand all the suffering around me, all the pain in the world. It's like I feel it all, I feel it lining my skin, lining my belly. I can't close my eyes to it. All I see is the pain everywhere.

The cosmic joke of it all, to suffer on a rock that is wasting away in a dark void, powered by a sun that will eventually burn out. What does it matter? It doesn't, it just doesn't, yet everyone is marching around pretending that it does, doing dumb shit like getting car insurance or planning their stupid engagement photos. And we're sending people to prisons to rot because of made-up rules upheld by a fearful majority, we're condemning X and celebrating Y, but it's all arbitrary and ridiculous. It's a parade of fools and there's no way out and I just want out. I don't want this. I don't want any of this. I don't want to feel like this anymore. I don't want to be here anymore. I don't want to be anywhere."

The tears have stopped by now. There is only a dead feeling left in my chest. I felt nothing but cold detachment from the world and from myself. Even the passion of the words I just shouted has left me. I simply feel … nothing. Boredom, perhaps. Whatever; she won't get it. No one ever gets it. Everyone prefers fiction, the comfortable lies. Everyone prefers to put on their blinkers and drown themselves in reality TV or Instagram, signalling to others that they are happier than they are, stuffing themselves with junk food and throwing it all up again. Half a world obese and half a world starving; people standing in front of monuments and pretending to feel something but really just taking photos that they'll never look at again. What is the point of trying to explain any of it?

This session is going to be just another waste of time. Another waste of an hour, a waste of a day, a waste of a life. Whatever. The sense of discomfort that I have always felt, that has been with me for most of my life, has intensified. Now I just want to leave.

While I spewed out my hateful words, Kate never broke eye contact. She kept with me as I took her on a tour of the darkness in my mind and soul, down into the hole that I had been digging myself into for so many years. She let me talk – or shout, rather – uninterrupted, unflinching, undaunted. She was present, calm, aware, alert.

Once she is certain that I have finished speaking, she says, "Well done. You have identified that there is suffering and injustice in the world. Do you think you're the first person to ever think this? Or say this? Or feel like this?"

I am shocked by her lack of sympathy and feel instantly infuriated. How dare she try to rob me of my rage? How dare she try to make my pain sound like everybody else's?

"Well, obviously not, but no one seems to care!" I shout.

"Everyone cares. They're just not as childish about it as you," she calmly replies.

What the fuck? I glare daggers at her. I can't believe what she's just said to me. And then, out of nowhere, I start laughing. It's so unexpected. She is giving me no pity; she isn't backing away in the face of my rage or deleting me or changing the topic. She is meeting me head-on – something that has never happened and which to this day is still rare. She is meeting my challenge, and she is winning. I have been caught off guard, so I just keep laughing. The laughter becomes almost hysterical, and suddenly I start crying. She lets me cry for as long as I need. I'm not sure how much time passes. It is probably only a couple of minutes, but it feels like a thousand years. I cry for all the pain I see in the world, all my wasted potential, my failures at school and university, my failed relationships, the bridges I've burnt with friends, the people I have betrayed and who have betrayed me, my utter sense of powerlessness to fix the world, the staggering extent of global problems, my loneliness.

The tears finally stop. I reach for the glass of water next to me. I down it all and wipe my nose.

Kate is still focused on me. "So, what's the plan?"

"I don't know." I sniff. "I just finished my undergrad. I guess I should do my honours or something next year. Keep stalling from making any serious decisions. I don't know what I'm doing."

Now Kate's voice is gentle. "I think you need to take next year off. And I think you need to work on yourself. A year just for you. A year for Alexandria. You commit to therapy, twice a week. You get into a routine of healing and calmness, and create wholeness. We create a structure for you to learn how to make peace with yourself and the world. Give it one year. And then, in a year's time, in December 2017, you pick it up again and take the next step."

I could say that I stopped my whole life between 2016 and 2017 to just do therapy, but I barely had a life to even stop at that point. In all honesty, I don't think I would have been alive much longer if I had continued on my own. It wasn't like there was no reason to live; it simply felt like there was no reason why I shouldn't die.

Many people who think they know my startup story believe I got the idea for DigsConnect as an undergrad student, miraculously built the platform at the start of my honours year and, next thing, had created a juggernaut and was a hugely successful founder. The truth is that wedged slap-bang in the middle of "got the idea" and "built the platform" is 2017, a year in which I tried to fix myself. And while that year of intense therapy brought me back from the precipice, it was just the first step in a long, long journey. It's a journey that I will be on for the rest of my life, trying to make peace with myself and the world and channelling my energy to deal with the existence of suffering, man's propensity for cruelty and the fallibility of human nature.

There is an ocean of sadness out there. I once thought that if I submerged myself deeply enough in it, I could fool myself into thinking that it had the answers or that I'd uncover some mystical truth, like some voyager in the dark, like Dostoevsky, Nietzsche or Plath who could all speak to the loneliest parts of my soul. I thought I could hold up my misery like a badge of honour, thinking it set me apart.

It doesn't.

There is no great truth in sadness. There is no honour in despair. Darkness will come throughout our lives. It's unavoidable. But what will also come, if we are open enough to receive it, is joy, peace, love, contentment, companionship and wonder.

In 2017, I realised that I had to decide whether I wanted to stay in the darkness or commit myself to the light. Like all things worth having, it took work – and continues to, especially if you are like me and a little prone to self-sabotage.

Kate was there to guide me but, like any psychologist,

she could only shine a torch on the path. I had to walk it myself. I had to put in the effort to drag myself out of the pit of my own miserable creation and back into the light. I had to choose to want to live and save myself. I realised that taking radical self-responsibility was the thing that would save me. It's the thing that will save us all. No one is coming. Heaven and hell exist only as states of mind. We can all claw our way out of that pit when we realise that our redemption lies in our own will to claim it.

Coming out of a hopeless depression is one of the most remarkable journeys a human can experience. It felt a lot like summiting Kilimanjaro. Suddenly, it was as if I'd woken up. I saw the dawn illuminating a new world. The sky got a bit lighter. The air warmed up a notch or two. I noticed that I was sitting on top of the mountain instead of staring up at it. I saw the expansiveness of the sky. I felt the sturdy earth beneath me. I saw the heavens surrounding me. I saw that nothing was everything and everything was nothing and that I would be fine, that everything was fine and would always be fine. It felt like I was finally awake.

So, *ja*, I got the idea for DigsConnect as an undergrad in 2016. In 2017, I took a year off to untangle my mind and learn to live with myself. Then I launched the website at the start of my honours year at UCT in 2018, and fate intervened to help me build what would become a fucking juggernaut.

CHAPTER 16

MEETING GREG

Around the time I'm campaigning to be SRC president, Uber has just launched on campus. The Uber rep at UCT is Greg Keal, a guy I know from the SRC. While I have run for office as a non-politically-aligned independent candidate, Greg is head of DASO, the DA Students' Organisation – not only for UCT but for the entire Western Cape.

He is pretty impressive. He started an NGO while he was still at school and trains fresh crops of DASO candidates, relentlessly driving them on the path to success. I, on the other hand, have no formal political background except for years of debating, fuelled by a lot of anger and a massive chip on my shoulder.

I'm not alone in these sentiments. Many young South Africans feel similarly pissed off. Perhaps that is simply the way most young people feel – disillusioned with power structures and ridiculously idealistic when it comes to solutions. When you're young enough to not really be invested in the system, it's much easier to want to tear it all down. That being said, not fighting and not voicing anger usually leads to the complacency of comfort, which makes many young people stodgy and far too accepting of things that need to be questioned and changed.

When the SRC results come in, Greg is among the top three candidates and one of the youngest SRC members ever to be elected. His campaign had been flawless. He'd practised his speech to the point where every inflection was precisely where he wanted it to be. He'd managed, at just the right time, to bring the rapt audience to tears and then elicit appreciative laughter when he made a joke that he knew would land. He'd run it like a military campaign, targeting the areas with the busiest foot traffic and placing perfectly designed election posters en route. Greg is also very good-looking, so the posters bearing large photos of his face had certainly drawn appreciative eyes.

While I was a ball of overexcited chaos with my blue hair and red coat, he was always meticulous and highly organised. He was like a shark tasting blood when it came to achieving his goals. To be honest, I wasn't sure whether I liked him. He was too cool; everybody loved him, and he was on top of his game, always. I was the complete opposite – either hitting a home run or missing the ball entirely, and always shooting from the hip. I never wrote a single speech. I would simply stand up in front of the crowd at rallies on campus, assess the mood and just speak about whatever was on my mind, whatever I thought the zeitgeist on campus was. Sometimes it was a bull's-eye and I had the crowd on tenterhooks, securing votes by the dozen. At other times, my game was so off that I totally misread the room and what I said fell flat. I could feel it. In the end, Greg beat me hands-down in the election, so clearly his strategy was far superior.

After we are appointed to the SRC, Greg and I slowly form a bond – first out of respect as we begin to understand the way the other campaigned. It becomes clear we share values and have the same vision for the future, underpinned by an unquenchable desire to make it work.

After a while, we start to really like each other once we realise we have the same sense of humour, the same larger-than-life approach to projects and a shared lust for life. But it is our mutual fondness for ice-cold G&Ts, which we drink sitting on the windowsill of his Sea Point apartment most evenings as the sun sets over the Atlantic, that really seals our connection.

By 2016, we are more than two decades into our democracy as the purported rainbow nation, yet poverty is not only rife but also increasing. A mixture of rage and hopelessness simmers in the bellies of the youth who were promised a better future and instead got a corrupt and bloated government.

Load-shedding was introduced as far back as 2007 in South Africa, but it feels like it really starts escalating when I get to UCT. It is a blight on our beautiful nation (and it has continued to get worse, right into 2024). But, as far as I'm concerned, of all the evils nipping at the heels of South Africans, the scourge of violence and rape is the loudest, vilest and foulest of them all. In 2016, while I am still on campus as a science student, it feels like every other week a new story breaks of yet another rape, of yet another dead woman, killed by her boyfriend, a rejected suitor or a crazed stranger. The rage and powerlessness that women feel becomes palpable in the streets. All these frustrations come to a head that same year when students protest in their thousands across campuses and at Parliament. Women have had enough! It is during this time that the #MeToo movement also takes wing across the world. GBV problems seem insurmountable and occupy our conversations at braais and digs parties and during coffee breaks between lectures.

It feels like I'm trapped in a world riddled with insecurities and complications, that I'm an unwilling participant and the inheritor of a complex history that I don't know how to piece together. I'm not alone. Millions of people are frustrated by the slow churning of corrupt power and circumstance. I am also acutely aware that I'm witnessing a great moment in history, this bubbling pot, the wheel of time turning, as I sit in my office on the top floor of the Steve Biko Students' Union Building on Upper Campus. The SRC offices line the top floor, and we look down across the campuses to the Cape Flats and beyond, out towards the Hottentots Holland mountain range marking the boundary of the "Republic of Cape Town".

Greg and I often climb out and sit on the roof of the Steve Biko building for the best view. We've figured out how to remove the burglar bars from the windows and dismantle the latches. Some evenings, we sit out there, nine storeys up, to smoke tobacco rollies and drink a whiskey.

I would be lying if I say that we sit on the roof of that historic building, on that historic campus at the preeminent university on the African continent, discussing lofty ideas and rhetoric like democracy, addressing poverty, geopolitics, the student housing crisis and the political landscape of South Africa. In reality, we mainly speak shit about everyone we don't like, and we think up ways of undermining them, laughing till we cry. Michelle Obama said: "When they go low, we go high." Well, we are happily going low.

We get on fabulously, laughing madly the whole time. Sometimes you just click with someone. Sometimes it just makes sense, and that's all there is to it. It just works. We connect on the most basic of levels. It feels like we are co-conspirators, dreamers, crazy enough to believe we are the ones who will change the world.

One evening on the SRC roof, Greg says that he has finally come out to his parents. Cape Town is generally regarded as an exceptionally liberal city, but South Africa as a whole is not. The private boarding schools we both attended were certainly not open-minded or liberal, which made it exceptionally hard to speak and live our truth as teenagers. And, while it was hard for our generation, it was almost unthinkable for our parents' generation, who were often staunchly conservative South Africans who simply never spoke of such things. But Greg speaks his truth, despite the bigotry and ignorance of others who try to bring him down.

During those early months after we meet each other, Greg and I just sort of become this "thing", without even trying. Straightaway we realise that with a single look, we know exactly what the other is thinking and feeling. There is an understanding between us, obvious and inalienable.

But what seals the deal on our friendship is something quite remarkable.

When I was at school at DSG, one of my closest friends was a girl called Liz. Liz had a cousin called Dylan Ramsay, who was at St Andrew's College, so I had known Dyl through Liz and from school since I was 14.

One afternoon, Greg sends me a message. It's a photo of him and Dyl. "My boyfriend says he knows you!" We all meet up and get on famously. We spend many evenings at our favourite pizzeria at the time, Posticino in Sea Point, eating pizza and drinking far too much wine.

Posti's is famous in Cape Town. It's always packed. It's been in the same spot for decades, and the pizza is incredible and affordable. There's fake Italian stonework painted onto the walls and the occasional archangel looking up exultantly, which becomes more hilarious and beautiful as you move on to your second and third bottle of wine. Greg and I make it our regular dinner spot. He lives up the road in Sea Point, which makes it extra convenient.

After dinner, Dyl and Greg go out and I head home to read or draw on my walls (I've drawn a huge mural around the entire apartment). Sometimes I just drive slowly around the Peninsula on my own. Often, I end up on Signal Hill. I park my car by the side of the winding road, get out and stand on the cusp of the hill, right where it falls away. The view is spectacular. It's iconic Cape Town. At night, Table Mountain is lit up with spotlights and looms huge and magnificent above the City Bowl. I take out a packet of tobacco, roll myself a little cigarette and watch the lights beneath me. Alone, as always; brooding, as always. Dissatisfied. Hungry. Itching for something, but not knowing what. A different world, a better world? Is this it? Is this all real? Is this our world, our country, our fate? Is this my life?

CHAPTER 17

CREATING DIGSCONNECT IN MY CHILDHOOD BEDROOM

Towards the end of 2017, after a year of talking my life through with Kate, I do what I always do when I need to recalibrate – I go deep into the wilderness. This time, it's to the Himalayas. I have just finished a Vipassana course, which remains one of the most intense experiences of my entire life. Probably even more than Kilimanjaro. Vipassana is 10 long days of silent meditation. It takes you deep, to your very core, and you have to be ready for what you find there. There's no contact with the outside, no contact with anyone at all, no distractions; just your mind and the boundaries that you encounter and push against.

After the retreat, I find it hard to readjust to "civilian life". The year is coming to a close and I need to make some decisions, so I seek refuge in Nepal, washing up in Kathmandu.

Every time I've landed in a new and foreign place, it's always *Ulysses*: *"I cannot rest from travel: I will drink*

Life to the lees ... I am a part of all that I have met; Yet all experience is an arch wherethro' gleams that untravell'd world whose margin fades ... As tho' to breathe were life! Life piled on life ... Come, my friends, 't is not too late to seek a newer world ... for my purpose holds to sail beyond the sunset, and the baths of all the western stars, until I die. To strive, to seek, to find, and not to yield."

Kathmandu draws me in and leaves me breathless, although that's probably partly to do with the exhaust fumes that thicken the air. Air quality aside, the city is everything I adore when I travel. I don't stick around, though, and a day or two later I catch a flight to Lukla, the most dangerous "airport" in the world, perched on a tiny strip of land on the side of a mountain.

My journey to the foot of Mount Everest is beautiful, full of peace and wonder (quite different from Kilimanjaro!). On the final day, I approach the foot of Sagarmatha, which means "goddess of the sky" in Nepalese, or Chomolungma, which in Tibetan means "mother goddess of the world".

I find myself high up in the Himalayas, having passed through valleys and past waterfalls, yaks and villages. On the final approach, gentle snowflakes float down from the sky. And here, at the foot of the highest peak on earth, snow falls softly around my feet, on the sleeves of my jacket and on my loose hair. Quietly, the rocks surrounding me turn white, blending in with the colossal glaciers along the ancient, soaring mountains around me. I walk on, away from the group with whom I was laughing and eating in the village just a couple of hours earlier. It is a moment to be alone. I arrive solo at the base camp as the light snow passes and the sky becomes blue and vast again, massive and clear and eternal. Again, I have found my place on this earth. I remember that the time in which I find myself alive is a gift that I can use to create something extraordinary for humanity and all that is yet to come.

Back in South Africa, I travel to the Eastern Cape to visit my parents before my postgrad studies kick in. I'm due to return to UCT in 2018. I keep wondering where I will live in Cape Town. I keep thinking of the tens of thousands of students who will soon arrive on campus, most in far more desperate predicaments than mine.

I know the story so well. Every year, students arrive on campuses all over the country with a dream of an education, but all too soon that dream leads to a dead end – to a sleeping bag in the library or in a campus bathroom. To uninhabitable hostels owned by unaccountable landlords. To impossible living situations that result in two-thirds of these students dropping out of university before they can graduate, rendering the tax money spent on their education obsolete and destroying their shot at something better than the anonymous drudgery of poverty. After more than two decades of democracy, is this the state of our nation?

The image of that shack erected by enraged students on campus in 2016 during the #FeesMustFall protests remains stark in my mind.

One December morning, I wake up at my parents' house in PE, clear my messy desk of the usual clutter and decide: today is the day.

I did a semester of computer science as part of my science degree, so I know the basics of hacking together a simple website. I rent a shared server from Hetzner for R30 a month. (I wish our servers still cost R30 a month!) and register the domain as www.digsconnect.co.za. I call it DigsConnect because "digs" is a common word used in South Africa for a student house, and "connect" because, duh, it's a marketplace. I mean, it's not exactly a revolutionary term; it's kinda obvious. (It also sounds suspiciously like "Dicks Connect", which I find hilarious.)

In between bouts of voracious snacking and annoying my little sister who is furiously texting her latest boyfriend 24/7, I spend the next two days creating an extremely simple two-page website. One page is to add a digs (property) listing, and one page is to view the digs listings. I create the logo on Microsoft Paint (literally) just by putting the word "digsconnect" over two lines. I come up with a colour scheme after scrolling through some of my favourite art Instagram pages, and I pick obscure colours with kooky names like "tequila sunrise" or "baby elephant's breath", mostly because they make me laugh.

Two days later, on a Sunday night in December 2017, after *Carte Blanche* and Derek Watts told us the state of the country and after the 8pm movie, I launch DigsConnect version 1 on the world wide web. I dreamed it up, I built it, and now it's real. Just like that. After years of fantasising, of dawdling and making endless excuses, after just two days of effort, suddenly it's real. And it was insanely easy.

What had really motivated me to get off my ass and just "do it" was a convo I'd had with a friend, George, who was a software developer at a tech startup in Silicon Valley. We had met in Maths 1000 at UCT. While complaining on a phone call about how hard it was to find student accommodation in Cape Town, I had offhandedly mentioned my idea for a platform where all the housing options could be listed and someone could simply log in and pick one.

"Then build it," he'd said.

Yeah right. "I don't even know where to start," I'd protested.

"Easy. Find a server, use this framework. It'll be up in a jiffy."

Back home for a long break in PE, which isn't exactly a metropolis of activity and wild distractions, I had plenty of time to think about it. And then, instead of just navel-gazing, I did it.

I return to Cape Town just before New Year, on 30 December 2017. I watch the sun come up above the horizon on New Year's Day from Dalebrook Tidal Pool in Kalk Bay and celebrate a new start with a chai latte. The tidal pool will forever be one of my favourite places on earth.

My phone buzzes. It's a message from Greg Keal.

"Proc, I heard you're back in Cape Town! Coffee next Tuesday?" God, this city is small. I wonder who else knows I'm back.

In the meantime, I keep watching my little website on Google Analytics. I notice that something crazy is happening. It's taking off! It's early January in Cape Town;

years later, we'll note that about 60% of our revenue comes in this month as students scramble to lock down their accommodation before classes start in February, but right now it feels like serendipity: the website has come to life at the exact time that people need it, so they've started using it.

As the days go by, while I sit on campus, meeting friends and getting ready to start my own classes, listings are cropping up all over the country. I feel more excited than I have in a long time. I have no idea what the word "entrepreneurship" even means other than what I've seen in films, and I certainly don't consider it a viable future. I don't even know the first steps to creating a business. But I'm having fun, so I think I can run this little DigsConnect thing as a side hustle while I get on with real life and embark on my postgrad studies. I then come up with a plan and email my lecturers, asking if I can do the honours stream in two years instead of one so that I'll have time to work on DigsConnect. The answer is a flat "no". I then go to the head of the department to plead my case. He also refuses.

Then I call George in Silicon Valley to discuss my dilemma. He simply says, "Drop out. Go for it, go back to varsity later."

On campus, I decide to go and see Dr Adam West, who lectures on botany and is my student advisor. He is one of the best lecturers I've ever had and has even won the highest teaching award at the university. When I tell him my idea, he says: "Try this DigsConnect thing. University isn't going anywhere. Your final marks are good enough to get you in this year or next year, but it seems you have something on your hands that is working. I say go for it."

(A few years later, I'll pop by his office to tell him all that came of DigsConnect after I followed his advice.)

Greg and I have made plans to meet up for ice cream on the promenade. He knew about DigsConnect back when I first had the idea. I now tell him that I have a working prototype – an "MVP", which is the startup word for "minimum viable product". I tell him I'm thinking of dropping out and working on it full-time.

"So, what's your plan? How do you see it working?" he grills me.

"Dunno, I just want to solve my own problem, really. Like, I'm back at university and haven't found a long-term place to stay yet. It would just be great to go on my phone and pick the best housing options."

That evening he calls me. "Meet me tomorrow at my flat, Proc. I have a proposition for you." Greg is in. I have a co-founder.

I sell him half of DigsConnect for R5. To this day I still have that R5 coin. It has the smiling face of Madiba looking at me from the wall behind my desk where I stuck it.

Our lives are the culminations of our decisions. Saying yes to Greg when he asked to join DigsConnect has been one of the best decisions I've ever made. In case you haven't picked it up yet, he's one of the greatest human beings on this planet.

A couple of days later, I'm back on campus. I have designed a super-simple poster showing an alien eating a slice of pizza. This is for no reason other than I think it looks cool. I go to the university library, print out as many as I can afford (probably about 100) and decide to stick them up around campus and hand them out.

Of course, this isn't my first rodeo when it comes to campaigning on campus. I did similar stuff during my SRC campaign, so I resort to all my old tricks. The less money you have for marketing, the more creative you can be. It's not a question of resources; it's a question of *resourcefulness*. And when all else fails and the chips are down, just do the craziest thing you can think of.

I have to somehow market my little website by relying on my utter lack of *skaam*. So, every morning, I go to every lecture theatre and log in on the computers. I change the background image to a DigsConnect poster so it will be the first thing that the students see in the lecture as the professor gets the slides ready. I pull every favour I can to get onto UCT radio and to put stickers on all the coffee cups in the food court, behind bathrooms doors, under toilet seats, behind bus seats, on all the walking routes that have the most traffic, in res during dinner, at digs parties and on my friends' social media pages.

I become obsessed with the website. Slowly, shakily, with one window on my laptop always open on CodeAcademy or some other free online coding tutorial, and another window open on my IDE (integrated development environment), where you write code, I figure out what I want to add to the platform and then simply add it. It often crashes in the process and I have to debug it while it is still live.

It's almost impossible to find a CTO (chief technology officer) and specifically a technical co-founder, when you can't afford to pay them. So the only solution is for me to be the CTO no matter how shit I am at it. It's a case of just getting get the job done. No excuses. Level up, figure it out.

At social events or dinners, or while sitting in on lectures, I take my phone out and watch Google Analytics, grinning as the traffic increases.

I soon notice that people I don't know, people I have never even spoken to, are signing up and creating property listings. I overhear students talking about it in the food court or on Jammie Steps between classes. Every time I hear DigsConnect being mentioned, I want to scream, run up to them and give them a full-on smooch of gratitude. Somehow, I restrain myself. I have no idea what is happening, but it's a feeling like nothing else in the world.

I really only wanted to fix a problem that was rocking my campus. But somehow, like Alice falling down the rabbit hole, I have tumbled headfirst into the role of creating … *something*. Whatever it is, it seems to be kind of working. It is exhilarating. It is electric. It's the feeling of finding myself in the place where I'm meant to be. After all the bad things that everyone always said about me, all the teachers and authority figures, the rules and regulations and the "how things are done", that world where I felt so out of place, out of step and disjointed, I suddenly have a role to play. I have discovered some sort of meaning, and now there is a harmony to life. Building this "thing" just felt so easy. It was a no-brainer. I had been a fish out of water, but now I'm swimming free and realising that I'm a damn good swimmer.

For years, I had agonised over who I was, what I was meant to be, what I was meant to do, what the right choices were and where I was headed. I had always been too scared to commit to anything in case it was the wrong thing. In a world of a billion options, where do you even start?

But I know now that if we allow ourselves, we gravitate towards the things we enjoy, and the things that we enjoy are generally what we're good at doing. Sounds obvious, but it doesn't feel like it when you're 23 and you lack the self-assurance to like what you like and be who you are.

I have realised that being good at something and enjoying it makes you an absolute killer. Whenever I'm asked to give advice to young entrepreneurs, I say: pay attention to what activities drain and bore you, and what activities energise and excite you. Chances are there's something in that, some hint or clue about your true calling.

With DigsConnect, I unknowingly followed my aptitude for audacity, spunk and stubbornness, which had previously gotten me into so much trouble. Now, it somehow works for me.

What I have unwittingly stumbled upon is value creation. I don't know this at the time, but business is essentially just the act of creating value, to the extent that someone (hopefully a lot of someones) will pay you for that value creation, exchanging value for value.

A few weeks after I launched the DigsConnect website, I find myself sitting in the old SRC offices, chatting to other members. I'm like, "Guys, I've built a website called DigsConnect, and I'd like your support to launch it on campus." But because I speak quite quickly, they are like, "Dicks Connect?! Are you sure we want to push this Dicks Connect agenda?"

I'm like, "No, guys. DIGS-Connect." By then, some guy

on the SRC has drawn a picture of two dicks touching at the head. He's like, "This has to be the logo for Dicks Connect." (On a side note, we'll end up buying the domain dicksconnect.com for a pretty hilarious marketing ploy.)

Greg and I redesign our campus marketing material and run campaigns for students saying: "Tag your digs pics @ digsconnect and get R100 on us!" You can just imagine what Instagram looks like the next day. It certainly raises a few eyebrows. We receive a bit of a backlash from the more conservative crowd, but just like everything else we do, the campaign gets attention. They say there's no such thing as bad publicity.

I remember sitting in a lecture, looking at our Google Analytics and thinking, "Wow, check our traffic! This is insane! Who are these people going on our platform?" The numbers are way higher than just the UCT crowd.

The original platform required students to sign up with their UCT email addresses. I reckon this was part of the reason why it worked so well in the early days. It was a closed community, with everyone just a couple of degrees of separation from each other. But soon my mates at other universities and colleges were also requesting access, so we then included email signups from other tertiary institutions.

Students from UCT, the Cape Peninsula University of Technology, the University of the Western Cape, Vega, Varsity College and AFDA are already using the website – and then listings from Stellenbosch, the closest university town to Cape Town, start to appear. I'm like, "This is hectic."

Somehow, it just works. Landlords create their listings and students contact them, and because it is all kinda intimate, people who know people, it seems to spread through word of mouth. There is something organic, safe and familiar about the site. Then, bang-boom-wham: the City of Gold, eGoli, our local big smoke, Johannesburg in bustling crazy Gauteng, a world away from laid-back, chilled-out Cape Town, comes on board. The universities there are humongous. In Joburg, there are skyrise student residences in their thousands and students in their tens of thousands. I'm like, "This is insane."

One day, Greg and I are sitting at the little desk we share when I get a phone call. (Greg, without telling me, has made my phone the official DigsConnect hotline and pasted my number on Google search, our Facebook page and our website. To this day, I still get random phone calls from people asking if they can come and stay at my house.) The caller is like, "I love what you guys have done with DigsConnect. I have 4,000 student beds and I'm going to list them all on your platform." This is our biggest single listing yet! We ask, "Are these beds around UCT's lower campus? Rondebosch or Claremont, perhaps?"

"No, Potchefstroom!"

Greg looks at me. "Where the hell is Potchefstroom?"

Quick googling ensues and we come across North-West University, with 75 000 enrolled students. *Jissis!* It dawns on me that this thing is much, much, much bigger than I ever imagined. "I wonder how much all these students are paying in rent?" I ask Greg.

We're like, "Holy shit. This is happening." The traffic is spiking exponentially. And while all of this is going down, I drop out of my honours programme and decide to focus entirely on the startup.

CHAPTER 18

DROPOUT

I know I'm no Silicon Valley hotshot, but the original DigsConnect platform I built is getting the job done. That being said, its first iteration is hideous. It is janky as heck, like a car that has been duct-taped together.

I remember a day when I spend hours working on what I consider to be the greatest new home page known to mankind. It has a bright yellow background. "That'll stand out!" I reason. In a white font, it says: "Student acomodation" (sic).

Feeling chuffed with my efforts, I spin my laptop around to show Greg. He lets out a bloodcurdling scream and drops his coffee all over the floor. "What the hell is that?" he gasps. "It looks like a Grade 4 project on the lifecycle of bees!"

Luckily Michael joins and becomes our CTO not long after. We then rebuild the entire platform from scratch in Django (a Python framework) and React (a JavaScript framework).

We host DigsConnect on Google Cloud because they give us a ton of free credits. (To this day, Google is still amazing at helping startups in South Africa. I can't tell you how much it helped – and still helps! – our cash flow to get credits for hosting, for ads and all the other services they offer. Amazon Web Services also does a pretty amazing job at supporting startups, and we probably would have hosted with them had they given us the credits first. Whenever we ran out of credits, we'd email Google and be like, "Hey, guys, want to give us more free credits?" They'd reply, "Yeah, sure." Absolute legends.)

Once the new platform is live, it just goes insane. I launched the first version of the website in January 2018, and within 18 months we're listing 70 000 beds on our platform in almost every city and town in South Africa with a major university or college.

We are bootstrapping – startup speak for being self-supporting. Greg has another business in logistics that he started before DigsConnect, so he is using that income to put his share of money into our business. I have no other business. One day when he is at my apartment, he says: "Proc, you don't need all this space." He knows that I need help with putting my share of money into Digs. Having grown up in the spacious Eastern Cape, my Cape Town apartment does not seem big at all. "Look," Greg continues, "if you put up a drywall along here and cut off the lounge, you could turn that into a bedroom."

Fuck it, I desperately need the cash. So, I borrow R20 000 to renovate, and within a week I have a room to rent out on DigsConnect. It's close to campus, so with a new roommate, I have an extra R4 000 a month to live off while we build the business.

A couple of thousand rand here or there allows us to

be creative, but worryingly, others have started noticing that we are onto something. Little copycat platforms start springing up. Marketplaces are a bit of a land grab, and you've got to grow fast. It would be oversimplifying it to say your value is down to one thing – it's much more nuanced and complex than that – but, essentially, if you don't have stock, you don't have a business. The best competitor is no competitor. We want a monopoly, so we have to move like lightning. This means we need cash.

In November 2018, we decide to let outside investors in. In startup speak, this is called the "seed round". You might also first choose to go the "pre-seed round" route – the "friends and family round" – and then you might have an "angel round", where a wealthy private individual may invest in exchange for equity. Once these pipelines are exhausted, then you usually move to the seed round. After that comes a "bridge round" (funding that's used to extend the runway of a startup until it can raise the next round of venture capital funding). Then, once things are up and running, there's a "Series A" round. Some people define this process by how much money has already been invested in the business, and some people define it by your revenue. But there are no hard-and-fast rules.

Once, after we have closed an investment round, I tell the media that it was our "seed extension pre-Series A round". A bunch of my founder friends text me saying, "What the fuck is a seed extension pre-Series A?" Who the hell knows? I make up the rules as I go.

In essence, we just need cash to move faster than everyone else who is trying to copy us. And that means selling part of the business (the equity) to venture capitalists. Venture capital is very high risk but comes with potentially very high rewards. Most startups fail, but a few go supersonic and, if you get in early at a low valuation, you are likely to be made for life. This is the gamble.

While startups in Silicon Valley and the EU can enjoy round after round of investment capital from venture capitalists, the VC market in South Africa is unlikely to carry you past a Series A if you are not self-sustaining, which is kinda brutal as you scramble for the holy grail of product-market-price fit in an unstable economy with not much spare capital among consumers. Regardless, once you understand the parameters, you realise you need to make money and make it fast.

Your role as an entrepreneur is quite simply to play within this space, to create a profit for your shareholders. Entrepreneurs are like the first movers in this game. I don't have a business background, so everything I know about business I learnt from doing it in real life. And it all comes down to value creation.

This is what the core of business – and, on a more fundamental level, the core of capitalism – is about, and why it's such a powerful force. Humans apply their abilities to generate value, and then we store, trade, speculate and swap value. Everything has a value. This value genesis and trade is what took our species from somewhere in the middle of the food chain to aiming for a base on Mars by 2030 (holding thumbs). It's why communism and socialism often fail: those systems seek to create value by dividing what already exists, instead of incentivising the creation of new value.

The US economist Walter E. Williams said: "Prior to

capitalism, the way people amassed great wealth was by looting, plundering and enslaving their fellow man. Capitalism made it possible to amass great wealth by serving and pleasing your fellow man." This encapsulates the near-reverence that I feel towards free-market economics and entrepreneurship.

By the time we meet our first investors, we've already had a couple of offers but we keep telling ourselves that we aren't ready. Then, suddenly, we are – and it's go time.

We put together our pitch deck. I soon realise that when it comes to fundraising, most of the work is in the preparation. If you prepare well and have your angle and your numbers, can justify your projections, have a reasonable budget and can convey your passion, vision and dedication, then things can happen.

The VC network is tough to break into. It truly is a game of who you know. This is obviously great if you know the right people, but we're outsiders – and initially it's a nightmare. My parents aren't in business, so even though I would have loved to rely on handouts, that avenue doesn't exist for me. And *ja*, sure, there are hundreds of websites for VCs that have big, shiny buttons that say: "Submit pitch deck here", which is basically a rubbish chute to a slush pile of pitch decks that some unpaid, 18-year-old BCom intern will summarily delete in between scrolling through hot girls' Instagram profiles. It's all about who you know. And we know no one.

When some things seem out of our control, we try to

focus on what we can control. In our case, there are tech meetups every week in Cape Town. I start religiously attending these and getting to know other founders. I post obsessively on social media to tell our story and build an online presence. I unashamedly DM CEOs and founders to ask for introductions. Almost all of them ignore me. Some even block me, but one or two agree to meet, which leads to three or four more meetings. We speak to friends who work in finance and tap into their networks with their older friends who work in finance. We meet anyone we can, telling our story repeatedly until we've honed our pitch, sensing what will be meaningful to investors, what will be a waste of their time and what will get us a second meeting.

We get some fantastic offers way sooner than we expect. Some of the potential investors even fly to Cape Town to see our office (the Love Shack). I notice their horror as the occasional rat runs in from the forest and skids across the floor.

By mid-December 2018, we have received incredible offers from big players in South Africa. We have almost closed a deal, with terms on the table, and are about to fly back to Joburg to sign the documents when we get a call from some guys who say, "We've heard about your startup, and we're in Green Point today. Can you come and meet us?"

To be honest, we really want to close the Joburg deal that is on the table. We debate whether to cancel this new meeting but finally agree to move our flight to later that day so that we can first attend the Green Point meeting. This is the right choice because it leads to us meeting our first investors and closing that historic R12 million seed round.

Within a week, our guys have prepped a term sheet. We run it by our legal advisors and close the deal a month later. In just five weeks, we have moved from an "initial chat" to a signed and sealed deal.

Our agreement with our first investors clearly lays out our targets for the next 12 months, so we throw everything we have at it. It's just grow, grow, grow – be big, huge, enormous, larger than large, bigger than a bull elephant bearing down on screaming tourists in a tiny rental car in the Kruger National Park.

Huge and roaring and unstoppable – that was 2019 for us. Looking back, it was one of the most fun years of my life. I was the young, newly minted CEO who had suddenly become the darling of the South African startup scene and, on paper at least, a self-made millionaire. Best of all, I was working alongside Greg, my best friend in the entire world, a one-in-a-billion guy, the kind of person who changed the lives of everyone around him. We laughed ourselves into tears most days as we ran as fast as we could. We had the tailwind. But here's the thing: we ran to win, sure, but we mostly ran because we loved the feeling of our own ability made manifest.

After I get my first-ever salary, I move into a gorgeous Camps Bay penthouse apartment surrounded by Glen Beach, the forest and Lion's Head. I spend every morning in the ocean and every sunset on the mountain. It feels like I am on top of the world.

We pull off more and more crazy marketing stunts, travelling the country as we take over. Every week we're on the radio, in the news, at another award ceremony. We stay in the office until the sun sets and the owls swoop low. We deck out the Love Shack with what feels like a million plants, and it looks like we're working in a jungle. We hire a team of fresh-out-of-university kids who are as crazy and ambitious as us, stock our fridge with beers and pizza and write quotes by Steve Jobs on the walls.

We release our DigsConnect app to the world one September morning at dawn after an all-night hackathon. Imagine our team of 12 or so 23-year-olds, exhausted, exhilarated, manic, baggy-eyed, pizza-greased, coffee-stained, barefoot and probably stinky as hell as the sun rises, finally typing in the commands to launch our app. The app hurtles to number one on the App Store for the whole of South Africa. This isn't down to luck but rather the result of a perfectly executed plan that involves student influencers across the country, crazy competitions and enough hype to start a revolution – all paired with our unbelievably talented app developer, who is back then still a full-time student.

And, my God, do we grow. From hundreds of users to thousands, then tens of thousands. We start experimenting with monetising our platform when landlords begin offering to pay to have their listings on the home page. And, because they get such fast results from student enquiries, an unintentional bidding war starts as they vie for that page. As we become more successful, I sense aggression from the old guard, the big boys in the space who have never been challenged before. They fly to Cape Town (usually from Johannesburg) to meet us in our dodgy little office, stepping gingerly over the debris on the floor in their expensive shoes and suits and making passive-aggressive threats about how they will crush us. Every threat is a badge of honour.

On one highly memorable occasion, a team member gets tapeworms and we all panic because we're prone to sharing food and not prone to a hell of a lot of office hygiene. We pile into Greg's car, speed down to the chemist and buy every dewormer in the place. We take entire boxes of the pills, chased by Red Bulls. Another time, our head of college partnerships, the ultimate workhorse, gets drastic food poisoning, refuses to go home in case he misses work – and then throws up ingloriously into our office sink, which remains clogged for weeks. Even after we get it sorted, it gives off a highly suspicious sour-carrot smell in summer.

And so, while we're deworming ourselves, laughing our heads off and cleaning sinks, we become the official accommodation partner for almost every single private college in South Africa. We are even integrated into their platforms. We walk into popular student coffee shops and see people with our stickers on their laptops. It's electric.

CHAPTER 19

DON'T DRINK THE KOOL-AID

In the early years of DigsConnect, I often tell myself not to drink the Kool-Aid, to differentiate between hype and traction, to create concrete value and not hot air. I feel immensely inspired by bold ideas, new technology, rampant and rapid innovation, moving fast and breaking things, "out with the old, in with the new". I tend to gravitate towards chaos.

However, with that first R12 million seed investment, we – especially me – convince ourselves that we've "made it". I am so caught up in being this 25-year-old self-made millionaire that I lose sight of the actual challenges. The investment money appears to be proof that our product is revolutionary and our brand iconic, that it embraces a social necessity – hell, it feels like we are the future of property! It becomes even more enticing to believe in our newfound power when one of South Africa's most eminent journalists, Bruce Whitfield, publishes a book claiming that Alexandria Procter and DigsConnect are a reason to be hopeful about the future of South Africa. He even tweets about me, saying, "Alexandria Procter is going to go far." Good God, can you imagine? My head expands to the size of a particularly large blue whale's left testicle (always the bigger of the two) and threatens to crush to death all who come within hearing distance of my bragging. All this naive hubris feeds the delusion of being untouchable.

If there's one thing I've learnt, it's that startups will humble you. I've learnt the hard way that the more I thought I was right, the less able I became to hear other opinions, which meant that I often didn't see the very real flaws and holes in our strategy. Over time, I've learnt how crucial it is to welcome critique, to go back a dozen times on a proposal to find the not-so-obvious problems and fix them. If your idea crumbles after a single criticism, it clearly wasn't very good to start with, and being unable to endure what might feel like a personal attack usually shows your weak spots.

While we have metrics in place, I always tell myself not to look at the vanity metrics. I read that phrase in some startup book, and it seems legit. In reality, I'm a total sucker for the hype. In those early days, we are off like a rocket, albeit a rocket that isn't too sure where it is going other than aiming for "1 million student placements". In all honesty, we have no clear plan on how to achieve that goal.

When a startup secures investment, like we did in 2019, there's all the fanfare and a veneer of glamour. While investment is of course important, it does not signify that a startup has "made it", that the business is necessarily working or that there is a product-market-price fit. Sure, receiving investment feels fantastic because overnight your bank account becomes bloated and you feel like the fat cat that got the rat *and* the cheese – the entire cheeseboard, in fact, and a bottle of French champagne to boot. But you allow complacency to sneak in when you're expanding your beautiful runway and hiring a huge, expensive (and usually unnecessarily large) team. And then there are the over-the-top launch events. Most of these things become meaningless when you're up against the wall.

A founder posts on social media that they have made a breakthrough with their conversion rate, released a new feature or figured out something tricky operationally, and the room yawns. A founder posts on social media that they secured $$$$ millions, and the room erupts with wild cheers. There's a reason why the saying goes, "Wisdom is never found in crowds." So many founders look at getting investment as the ultimate symbol of their company's success, but raising funding should be their very, very, *very* last resort.

The truth that no founder wants to hear is that revenue is the best investor. It's hard, but ultimately revenue is the only metric that counts. Customer adoption and traction that shows users are getting enough value from your product, a product for which they're willing to give up their hard-earned money – that should be your only goal.

There's a beautiful phrase in startup lore: "Do things that don't scale." It's like the wizard of Oz behind the curtain. While the front of house looks shiny and gleamy, it's almost always going to be a shitshow backstage while you scramble to make it work. That's the process; that's normal. You shouldn't have all the answers when you start because then it means you won't listen to your users. Build something, be destroyed by the critical feedback, and rebuild. Create value for your users and they'll pay you. You don't need gazillions to do this. It's highly unlikely that there isn't something you can do to get customers just by being scrappy.

There are so many epic stories of startups that did the wackiest things in their early days and used the most menial processes just to deliver results to their customers, all in a data-gathering exercise to figure out what the heck they actually had to build once their customers had shown them what *they* needed. Once that part is done and you've got a few customers, you're ready to build and you think that you absolutely need money for this part, then perhaps it's time to consider raising funds. But be warned: once you take money from other people, you're on the treadmill and there's no getting off.

Also, once you've raised funds, it's never enough. Soon you're in the inferno of your next fundraising, answering inane questions from finance bros who are fresh out of university and doing an internship organised by one of their dad's friends. Despite not having worked at a startup, they'll think they have superior, godly wisdom and feel compelled to share dreadful opinions that they got from listening to the *Rich Dad Poor Dad* podcast at the gym that morning.

As an early-stage founder with no cash and desperate to grow a talented (and expensive) team and pump operations and marketing, a couple of million dollars can look like the solution to all your problems. But equity is expensive. Money is, in fact, cheap and transferable and can come from a variety of sources, but equity is a one-off: once you give it away, it's gone. And it's almost impossible to get it back unless you manage to sign an incredible agreement, which is unlikely for a first-time founder. I always remind myself that we don't need the investors; we can get money anywhere. The investors, however, need us – founder-led companies outperform companies with hired CEOs nearly all the time.

I've also gradually came to realise that venture capitalists do this all day, every day; it's their full-time job to cut deals, whereas looking for funding is only a fraction of my job as the founder. They will most likely be better at this than you are, and some of them might try to screw you in some way. I've learnt not to sign anything until we had the best legal eyes on the contract – obviously always making sure they are our lawyers and not the investors' lawyers!

In a heady rush of youthful arrogance, we pursue growth above all else and apply our efforts to the areas where we feel rewarded. Initially, it looks like it is working. Our marketing and brand creation are, dare I say, iconic. We pull off insane stunts and achieve our goal of becoming a household name, the de facto platform for student housing in South Africa. Almost every student at the major universities knows about us and loves us because we are young, fun and genuine with a cool product UI. We partner with key institutions and land massive clients. I am invited to speak at conferences on themes ranging from property and blockchain to women in business.

I guess the saying is true – when the student is ready, a teacher appears. And so it is during this time that I meet someone who will have a significant influence on me.

CHAPTER 20

PRESIDENT PROC

From as early as I can remember until late into my teens, when anyone asked me what I wanted to be one day, my answer was instant: "I'm going to be the president of South Africa."

It was obvious to me. Being the top dog seemed like the best way to change the world. I naively believed that if I were president, I would just snap my fingers and all the suffering would be gone, and life would be a beautiful adventure for everyone. We'd all have a big laugh and eat choc-chip cookies while watching *Pokémon* on SABC 3, or maybe we'd just climb trees. I felt like if I were calling the shots, there'd be no waiting for someone else to make things happen (who would probably never get them done).

Then I grew up and saw the ineffectiveness of global politics: citizens being beholden to a party of self-serving bureaucrats, interested only in their own job security, serving short-term goals in a system designed to incentivise empty promises solely for re-election purposes. I realised that the work I had dreamt of doing wasn't going to come from that mess.

Despite my disdain for the system, there have been a few times when I have been pulled into politics. I can't quite help it. I deeply believe that, especially in developing economies, the public sector's involvement and personal investment in daily life is crucial when it comes to wrenching millions of people out of poverty. Business moves faster than public policy, and when public policy fails, we see the worst of business and the extortion of the vulnerable. But value genesis by highly incentivised, fast-moving entrepreneurs is crucial for humanity's progress. However, for this to work, we need whip-smart, highly motivated and incentivised policymakers to ensure no one is left behind. There's a phrase I like: "The future is already here; it's just not evenly distributed." The intersection of tech, startups, entrepreneurship, public policy, economic development, governance and leaders who inspire us to be better fascinates me and draws me in to explore my role in it.

In 2019, in the early days of DigsConnect, I am selected for the Democratic Alliance's Young Leaders Programme. It is a fantastic platform to explore these ideas.

Just like when at first I didn't make it onto the SRC, I am just below the cut-off point on the list of those who have made it onto this highly competitive programme. Because I am not active in politics and leaning more into my startup, others who are working in government have been prioritised. Thankfully, I have learnt from my mistakes when I didn't get onto the SRC, leaving me embarrassingly sulky. I also meet the programme assistant to run through my interview and see what I can improve in case there is a next time.

Then, a couple of weeks before the programme starts, I receive a call from the programme manager saying that one of the candidates fell pregnant and wants to focus on her pregnancy over the next year. So, once again, I'm in. When I get the call, it is 11am and Greg is sitting next to me in our little office. We promptly run downstairs, and he buys me a bottle of champagne. We down the whole thing and get rather festive. It's a good day.

Part of the programme includes being assigned a mentor from the party, usually a member of Parliament who has the time to give focused, one-on-one guidance. When I receive an email from the organiser telling us that our mentors will be assigned in the coming week, I don't want to get saddled with a (no offence, *mon amie*) 20-something-year-old parliamentary backbencher with about as much decision-making experience as an ant. I have no time to waste. I'm not going to sit around like a ninny waiting for my piece of cheese. I have to take matters into my own hands and find someone as ferocious as me. In my youthful arrogance, I believe that the only person fit for the task is Helen Zille: party leader, international political icon and a tad divisive, as most big-name politicians are. She is also the premier of the Western Cape, the ex-mayor of Cape Town and one of the most powerful people in the country.

I toy with the idea of trying to contact her on social media, but I know I won't stand out from the thousands of others vying for her attention. I know I can't go through official party lines because they will refuse. Gatekeepers always say no, which is why the only option sometimes is to parachute over the supposed boundaries special ops style and find your own way in. I'm firmly a member of the "ask forgiveness, not permission" camp. Otherwise, how the hell are you supposed to get anything done?

I need a more strategic approach that would make her think I am worthy of her time.

As the premier of the Western Cape, Helen lives in a state residence, Leeuwenhof, at the top of Gardens in Cape Town's City Bowl, bordering on Higgovale. It's a well-known landmark, and I've been there before for a Saturday-morning organic market (a very Cape Town activity). As usual, Greg is there to think the plan through with me because his victories are my victories and mine are his. We win together and we lose together in every business, project, undertaking, investment, plot, scheme, launch, venture, revolution or coup we embark on. *Upstart* isn't just my story; it's ours.

As we chat, an idea forms. We decide that I should drop off a huge bouquet at her residence with a well-crafted letter stuck in them, stating my case as a newly appointed DA Young Leader in need of a mentor. I imagine that the flowers will catch her attention long enough that she will consider reading the letter, and the letter will explain why I'd make a superb mentee.

Standing in the supermarket checkout queue with the bouquet, I see a newspaper headline about the water crisis in Cape Town: "DAY ZERO APPROACHES!" So, I decide on a whim that it would be more prudent (and witty, dare I say) to get her a water-wise succulent, ideally from the Karoo or somewhere equally patriotic.

I buy a little Karoo aloe, attach my letter about how we can change the world together, scribble down my contact details, climb into my banged-up old Mahindra Thar and drive up to Leeuwenhof. (I haven't yet bought my Mini, Angela Merkel, at this point.)

I have no idea what to expect. In high-intensity moments, a strange calm descends on me, and I drop into what feels like a natural mode of operating. My mind is usually racing frantically in a million different directions at a gazillion miles per hour, but when the heat is on, I get tunnel vision and become completely calm. I just get the job done, whatever it takes. In a way, it's similar to how I felt on the slopes of Kilimanjaro.

So, there I am, en route to Leeuwenhof, aloe strapped in on the passenger seat next to me. I drive up Kloof Street, turn left, then turn right, go up the little side street and arrive at the big front gates. Standing guard are a couple of members of the South African police force. It will be obvious in retrospect that the police would be on duty at the premier's official abode, but now I just have to wing it. They see me approaching and stop me, looking rather grave.

Then one of the cops spots my Eastern Cape registration plate and cracks a big smile. "Eastern Cape?" he asks. "PE!" I reply, grinning. "Mthatha!" he responds. Huge grins spread across our faces in the way that you smile when you meet someone from home in another corner of the world. Instant camaraderie.

We launch into an excited chat about our home province, laughing and cracking jokes.

"So how can I help you?" he asks.

"Well," I begin, "I'm on the DA's Young Leaders Programme, and I've come to drop a note off for the premier."

Luckily, I have a hard copy of the letter with the DA letterhead confirming I have been accepted. I explain my plan to the cop, and he listens, laughing when I say how I don't want to get stuck with a backbencher because I am planning to become president in a couple of years' time. I say he shouldn't laugh because I'm not joking, and he nods gravely. I ask him if I could just leave the plant and letter at the gate.

He looks at me with a glint in his eyes and a conspiratorial smile. Then he says, "Let's go leave it at her front door!"

God, this is why I love this country. We make things happen here, we get on with it; everything is possible if you're willing to give it a go. I have travelled extensively, and I can say with conviction that in any other country, there would have been a fuss with forms and protocol up to your eyeballs – enough red tape to ensure that no one ever tried to reach beyond their station or do something racy that might result in something extraordinary. South Africans are not a breed known for toeing the line. We put our feet, and then our entire bodies, right over the line, and then we make it work.

He jumps into my car and opens the gate. I put the old beast into gear and, tyres screeching, we race up the hill. I come to a juddering halt and pull up the handbrake. Then I place bricks behind two of the wheels, just in case, because the handbrake is about as reliable as Eskom's power supply. That makes the cop laugh even more. He tells me to leave the plant at the door, and then he walks off back to the gate.

Alone in the little parking area, I approach the front door and see, to my surprise, that it is standing wide open. Because of the high crime rate, South Africans hardly ever leave their doors open. I knock loudly and shout, "Hello?!"

a couple of times. I hear voices, and then a woman calling out, "We're in the kitchen!" Crikey. By now, I'm a little damp under the arms and feeling incredibly sheepish. This is the premier of the Western Cape! She won Best Mayor in the World two years earlier, and here I am, waltzing in through her front door with a bloody pot plant in my hands.

I step over the threshold onto a beautiful wooden floor, turn left and walk through a breakfast room into the kitchen. Standing there is none other than Premier Zille, having a cup of tea with her daughter-in-law and grandchild. She looks up at me, unflappable and amused, and simply says, "Hello there, who are you?"

"Oh, hey!" I say, as sheepish as the shyest sheep in the shed. "My name is Alexandria Procter, and I've come to give you this water-wise aloe and ask if you'd like to be my mentor for the DA's YLP." I hold out the plant, stiff-armed, as proof, waiting for the alarm to be triggered and to be carted off in handcuffs straight to Pollsmoor to share a cell with the 27s gang.

Almost instantly, Helen replies: "I'd love to be your mentor!" Oh my God, I can't believe this worked. Filled with glee at the thought of having once again ignored protocol, doing it my way and somehow pulling it off, I smile widely and relax.

"Would you like a cup of tea?" she continues.

"That'd be great, thanks! Earl Grey, milk, no sugar." I pull out a chair and help myself to a rusk on the table.

We hit it off immediately. Over the next 20 minutes, we get to know each other and lay out a plan for the mentorship. Then she says she needs to attend an event at some ambassador's house and finish some or other task that has to do with running the province. As she walks me back to my car, I notice a beautiful grand piano in the main lounge. I've been a piano player since I was a child, and to this day I still create tiny compositions that I post on social media. I comment on it. Helen then tells me that no one ever plays the piano and that I am welcome to come and practise on it. That's how I end up spending many afternoons tinkling on the piano at Leeuwenhof and learning about leadership from Helen Zille.

Between working on DigsConnect and being mentored by Helen, I continue with my governance work. I set up a small NGO focused on digital literacy and internet-based entrepreneurship in the townships. On weekends, my team and I base ourselves in the township public libraries that I have partnered with and run workshops on the variety of opportunities available in these historically opportunity-scarce places.

And then, just as things are going swimmingly on all fronts, disaster strikes.

Almost a year to the day after signing that R12 million seed deal, just as we are taking off into the stratosphere of success, a tiny virus called Covid-19 appears out of Asia. It causes a worldwide pandemic and global pandemonium. Life as we know it is about to change drastically.

On 27 March 2020, DigsConnect goes into hard lockdown along with the rest of South Africa. More than two years of harsh regulations are about to decimate the economy. The property sector is one of the hardest hit. Along the way, we will lose more than two-thirds of our team, including our CTO; lose our revenue; lose many of our clients; and stare down the barrel of the death of our company.

CHAPTER 21

A GLOBAL CRISIS

In early March 2020, on the evening that President Cyril Ramaphosa is due to deliver his very first live broadcast to South Africa about the coronavirus, the residents in my neighbourhood are already on high alert after thick smoke has been spotted on Table Mountain.

It's the end of a dry summer and high fire season in Cape Town. As residents of this beautiful city, we live with the permanent threat of wildfires. Most years, a vicious inferno will ravage certain suburbs, engulfing roads and houses in its path.

Now, as the sky grows darker, huge red flames are visible from the highway. Orange lines streak across the mountain. I am living on the very edge of the Camps Bay glen, the last property before the fire line. From my kitchen window, I watch the flames lick ever closer down the mountain.

There are three roads in and out of Camps Bay, and one is already engulfed in flames. The second is about to be closed off. This means that there's only one route out of the suburb into the city. Anticipating chaos, with the smell of smoke in the air and the reflection of flames in my windows, I pack a small bag of essentials. I'm literally choosing to leave behind almost everything. As I scan my apartment, I'm reminded of how quickly we get bogged down with so much clutter, baggage, dust, excess – sticky and too cloying for comfort.

Don't get me wrong; I loved the apartment. I loved its ambience, my bizarre collection of artefacts and curiosities, my art, my plants and my hundreds of books on shelves and windowsills and forming piles on the floor, but there's an inevitable neuroticism that comes with ownership. This applies to both stuff and people, because like many humans, I have a tendency of laying claim to those I purport to love. This feeling is subtle and devious because it can be mistaken for safety. But that's the delusion – because there is no real safety in life. There is no one coming to save you. There is nothing that can "fix it all". Terrible things happen every day, yet we distract ourselves with *panem et circenses*, with insurance schemes and interactions with central banks, ruled by an unconscious fear of our own mortality. I have come to believe that facing the inevitability of one's own death and rejecting the false veil of safety is the route to the deepest form of inner peace. A state of acceptance, when all is observed and all is welcomed. I read once that the trick to life is to die before you die and then realise that there is no death. I don't know if that makes much sense, but something in it feels true to me.

I don't know how much of this Zen rationality crosses

my mind the night of the fire as I scour my apartment, considering that all of it could be engulfed by flames within the next hour or two. I am just eager to get out of there. Carrying my MacBook, phone, passport, a change of clothes and my journal, I get into my recently purchased red Mini Cooper, aka Angela Merkel, and drive towards Greg's place on the only road still open. Flames dance in my rear-view mirror. I turn on the radio just as President Cyril Ramaphosa begins to speak: "Fellow South Africans…" The phrase will become ubiquitous thanks to his regular "family meetings" over the next 18 months.

As he speaks, I'm stuck in a line of cars winding its way along the oceanside pass, out of the burning suburb. Our mountain is on fire. As the president informs us that the world is about to change, more radically than anyone alive has ever experienced, I hear the wail of firetrucks going in the opposite direction. None of us have a clue just how bad this is going to get or how long it's going to last, but there is something sinister in the air.

I finally arrive at Greg's flat where I'm spending the night. Almost immediately, we get into action mode. The country is still open for business, and we have plenty of work to do. We are in the middle of hockey-stick growth, and we have to keep pushing. I am due in Joburg in a few days' time for a series of meetings with large-scale property developers. I'm also set to do a potentially big investor pitch. In line with our growth, we are planning to raise our Series A investment round at the end of the season, in June or thereabouts, so I am gearing up for that. We have been marketing DigsConnect heavily, which comes with a hefty bill, and we need to secure new investment to extend our runway.

The following morning, I wake up at Greg's place to discover that the fire is under control and my apartment has survived. Relieved to still have a home, I return to Camps Bay, and a few days later I'm on a plane to Joburg. The mood is a bit tense, with Covid-19 the only topic of conversation in the airport lounges, in Ubers and during small talk before my meetings.

Everyone seems nervous, but no one more so than the potential investors. On the third night, after an early dinner with a friend, I'm back in my Airbnb and I see a bunch of messages on my phone. "Turn on the news now!" On eNCA, I watch our president once again addressing the nation, this time announcing a 21-day nationwide lockdown.

Lockdown? What does that word even mean? We will learn soon enough. My remaining meetings are cancelled as people scramble to figure out where they will be bunkering down for the next three weeks. We have two days to sort ourselves out. I book a flight back to Cape Town. I manage to get the last seat on the plane. It's chaos at the airport.

CHAPTER 22

LOCKED DOWN

The first wave of lockdown reality hits our business when a slew of accommodation cancellations come through. Schools and university campuses are shut, and students are told to go home. Landlords lose leases by the thousands. Many of them now can't pay their suppliers, one of whom is us. Our revenue projections and trajectory for what looked like a sterling year collapse. This is obviously unanticipated. While we have a carefully managed budget and runway, we have been generously spending to secure a market land grab, hiring fast and accruing heavy expenses.

Before March 2020, we had plenty of runway, projecting our cashflow to be healthy with the seasonality of our business (along with hot investor interest). This made us feel extremely secure. Perhaps overly so. Overnight, everything changes. The pandemic feels eerily like the meteor and the dinosaurs, when those who were the rulers saw their environment change completely and, failing to adapt, became museum relics.

Next to go is the hot investor interest. No one is spending. The market crashes, people are retrenched worldwide in their millions, and businesses start hoarding cash until they know the full scope of the crisis. The prop-tech industry crashes. Two of our local competitors throw in the towel, essentially making DigsConnect the de facto rentals startup in South Africa. We're handed the monopoly we had always wanted, but it feels like a shot from a sawn-off shotgun because we, too, are in an accelerating downslide. We're unicycling like circus bears on a knife's edge, juggling the lives of our team members and our investors' resources as we try to find our footing.

On the one hand, we have our investors' and shareholders' interests to consider; on the other, our employees' interests as well as those of our clients and users are top of mind. Ideally, we want our work to benefit everyone. But when Covid-19 hits, it feels like helping one group comes at the expense of the other.

I've never really been a panicky person. So, with a couple of dark jokes laced with our morbid sense of humour, Greg and I come up with ideas for a way out of this. I've always believed that creativity is best expressed when conditions are the most constrained. As the count of Monte Cristo tells his (unknowing) son, *"Life is a storm, my young friend. You will bask in the sunlight one moment, be shattered on the rocks the next. What makes you a man is what you do when that storm comes. You must look into that storm and shout as you did in Rome. Do your worst, for I will do mine! Then the fates will know you as we know you."*

We start working on our budget, slashing line items

like Jack the Ripper on full tilt. Instinctively, I know that the first step in getting through this crisis is to stem the flow of money leaving the business. Like almost every participant in the economy, we are locked into contracts and commitments that cannot be reneged upon. However, everything can be negotiated.

I plead, beg and threaten our way into receiving massive discounts on our servers and office rent. I negotiate payment plans. I do everything I can to keep paying salaries and serving our customers so that we can carry on getting returns for our investors. I am a woman possessed.

The first rule of business is: don't run out of money. And as Warren Buffett told us, "The second rule is, don't forget the first rule." All my mentors have told me that when the bank account is empty, it's curtains. What I discover during this time is that, in fact, a business dies when the founders run out of energy. At DigsConnect, we've gone from a state of abundance and growth to a state of war. Overnight. And now it's a case of fight or die. We choose to fight.

Once we have cut the budget to the absolute minimal spending to keep the lights on, we need to bring in cash.

We are forced to re-evaluate our business model. We have until now been working on a freemium model, with about 95% of our users on the free tier. We kept to this model because, as a marketplace, we argued that we needed volumes in order to remain viable. We had vague plans to convert these users later, but in this new and treacherous world, any user who is absorbing spending but has no potential to yield revenue is a luxury we can no longer afford. And so, in the midst of the pandemic, we realise that we have to pivot our model.

It's crazy. The arguments within the team are some of the worst we have ever had. Landlords across the country are bleeding, and now I'm saying that they have to pay to use our services! The team thinks I have lost the plot. The situation is made worse by the fact that these incredibly tough conversations are happening remotely. Our team has never worked remotely. We soon discover that on video calls, there's no vibe, no connection, none of the bantering or spontaneity that we had shared in our little office where we would sing about the future, arms wrapped around each other in joy. Now we are sitting on our laptops, locked away, terrified and isolated, and on top of it all, I am proposing to change the business model radically overnight – yet again.

A business rests on its model. Around the model, you build the product. Around the product, you communicate the marketing. No matter how brilliant your marketing or how flawless your product, the business dies if the model is off. Our runway is growing shorter by the day. If the plan backfires, it will mean the death of our business.

But I am insistent. So, we begin working on the pivot that will either save us or destroy us. Greg and I divide the team up into small task teams, and everyone is given a part of the project to work on. As a seasonal business, our budgeting stretches as far as the start of the new season, which usually kicks off in September, peaks in January and ends in late March. We have just enough money to keep going until January 2021, which would have been perfect in pre-Covid times.

The team gets to work, grateful that things are moving forward again. We aren't sitting around and waiting for the axe to fall. We are super-busy, and that feels like progress.

By September 2020, we are still in lockdown with no hint of the world returning to the one we knew. Bookings are at zero. Things are feeling extremely dicey. Greg and I have Zoom calls from opposite sides of the country. Sometimes we talk, and sometimes we just sit in silence. The previous month, we had sent out comms to our users about the pivot, informing them that free DigsConnect would be phased out and everyone would need to pay a "booking" fee on placements. We lose hundreds of users almost overnight, and team morale takes another hit. It feels like we are walking to the guillotine.

What I soon notice, though, is that the users who have left the platform are those who never really responded to messages from students, those whose listings were incomplete or shoddy, and those who had a dodgy vibe about them. I decide that their exodus is a good thing for the business and that we should only represent users who put some effort into participating on the platform.

The product is manoeuvring into a new position, and something about it feels right. To me, it makes a lot more sense, this new model, this reduced suite of features for our users after we cut almost all other functionality that didn't directly help students book rooms. It feels simple, clean and streamlined. It reminds me of that Picasso sketch – you know, the one of the bull? He starts out drawing a super-detailed bull and then reduces it to a few simple lines that portray the very essence of the bull and conveys everything – perhaps even more.

After I've poured my heart, soul, blood, sweat, tears and every ounce of my life's energy into making this work, seeing it flow so beautifully thrills me deeply. I *knew* it would work. I knew it. We just have to ride out the storm. I know that if we just get a break, this startup will make it.

By November 2020, the minister of education has announced that he does not know when universities will be reopening. Our season looks like it might not happen. Not one booking comes through. Then, one of the investors we have been working with, doing due diligence, calls to say that he is out. The others just stop replying to our emails. The end of the runway is looming dark and large, a Mordor on my horizon. Things are getting scary. At this stage, we are experimenting with anything to bring in cash. Google Ads on the site? I abhor them on other sites, but right now I'll do whatever it takes: banner ads, ads on our map. (Usually, I wouldn't recommend tarnishing one's product in this way, but this is a war for survival.) We somehow extend our runway for another month. Let's keep going.

We also have a large and committed user base and, by working with a couple of corporates in South Africa, we run some platform marketing and lead generation to buy us an extra month or two. The rest of the team hates it – becoming a marketing platform is everything we have stood against, and it feels like I am betraying them. But we have to keep trying everything to keep the lights on. However, trying to justify why we are "selling out" is hard.

A startup is high risk. Everyone knows that. Runways are usually tight, and cash-flow management is an art. In the early days, the soul of the startup is the soul of its founders; its energy is your energy. There must, of course, always be substance, but because you are fighting insane odds (95% of startups fail within the first 12 months) and huge, wealthy corporates, sheer hype often keeps the ship going.

I have a childhood memory of watching a cartoon in which some characters are flying in a plane. They run out of gas, but the one guy has drunk so much whiskey that when he burps into the tank, the alcohol content on his breath powers the plane. (Kids' cartoons in the 90s were wild, man. I don't think they'd let children watch drunks fly planes nowadays.)

It's a ridiculous analogy, but it kinda feels like that's what's happening at DigsConnect as 2020 grinds to an end. It feels as if our sheer willpower is keeping this thing alive. When the willpower and the hype start to dip, the team senses it. That kind of negativity is highly infectious. It spreads like cancer, and people start to scatter. Demoralisation spells death for startups. No matter how bad it gets, you can never, ever show defeat as a founder. You have to manage your shit and have your game face on, no matter what's going on.

By this stage, things have gotten seriously bad with regards to our cash flow. I am stuck in a dilemma. The team must know when they need to start looking for other jobs. We are at the height of the Covid-19 lockdown in South Africa, and jobs are scarce. Our team is a group of brilliant, hand-picked and highly skilled individuals, but even the best tech companies worldwide are retrenching. I know I must give them enough time to find good jobs elsewhere. On the other hand, if I share just how mind-numbingly, soul-crushingly and spirit-defeatingly bad our situation is, the team will immediately scatter and we will be finished. I have many faults, but one of my gifts is my ability not to panic in a crisis. I think at my most brutally clear and focused during challenging times. Something about being in the fire clears my usually scattered mind and I go into war mode.

Most of my close friends at this point are other founders and tech CEOs in South Africa and abroad whom I'd met during Y Combinator's Startup School, an American technology startup accelerator. I now have honest conversations with the ones I trust most about team members they'd love to have on board. I ask if they will hire them with a week or two's notice should the need arise. This means that everyone on the team has some kind of insurance policy should things go completely tits-up. The team's welfare has been a massive point of stress, and sorting this out means I can devote more mental space to getting the company back on track.

Our landlord user base is in sheer panic as they face the prospect of another year of empty assets. Students are in a panic too, not knowing when or how they will resume their studies, and the investors are bleeding money everywhere. But at least we have solved the issue with the team. And just as I find some welcome headspace to move on to the next issue, the biggest blow yet hits with full force – one of the worst situations a founder can face.

CHAPTER 23

POACHED

It's not for everyone, this startup life. While the concept is often glamourised, the reality can be, as Elon Musk puts it, "like chewing glass and staring into the abyss". For every Brad Pitt or Amitabh Bachchan, there are tens of thousands of actors queuing outside casting rooms, waiting tables and wasting their talents on menial tasks as their dream drifts away. For every Steve Jobs, there's that guy whose name we can't remember who left tech in the early days, and hundreds of thousands more for whom something was just a bit off: the team, the model, the market or maybe just the timing (ouch, BlackBerry). For every Che Guevara, there are millions of nameless dead soldiers. For every JK Rowling, there's a multitude of unpublished authors, words lost in journals that no one will ever read.

The media focus on the glamour and the success stories, so kids pin up these heroes and victors caught in a moment of glory. They never show the ocean of drudgery, tedium and hopelessness surrounding that moment.

It's now deep into the second year of the pandemic. Every day feels like a lie; all of us behind masks covering overwhelming fear. I'm scrambling to find solutions, to find the answers, quell the exhaustion and energise the team, our investors and our clients.

Then, one day, Michael, our CTO and cofounder, decides to leave. Things have been growing increasingly tense between the two of us. I've considered him to be a great friend, maybe even my best friend. Months ago, as we sat on the side of Kloof Corner as the sun set, drinking beer, he'd told me that he loved me. It was entirely platonic, but we felt closer than siblings. We've spent every other weekend playing tennis, shovelling ramen down our throats or skating down the promenade. Yes, it's been slightly complicated because we dated briefly before he joined DigsConnect, but that was two years before. I trust him completely.

However, as we sink deeper into lockdown, tensions run high. Strain can bring out the best or the worst in people. When the going gets tough, the tough get going, yeah? While the stresses of the lockdown bring Greg and me closer to each other, banding together to form an indivisible unit, it's not the case with our CTO. The disagreements about the way forward become ugly, bitter and toxic. Personal jibes and old resentments flow between us. Worst of all, we sometimes have epic fights in front of the team. And founders must never, ever have ugly blowups in public. It destroys morale and any confidence the team has in your leadership.

However, not once has the thought of jumping ship crossed Greg's mind or mine. It isn't even a possibility. It's this, all the way to the end, no matter what. Punch after punch after punch – bring it on.

It's been a particularly tough week when the steel-toed boot of hard times lodges firmly up our arses. Our CTO asks Greg and me to meet him in our boardroom. He's holding a white envelope. "Look, I think you guys know what this is."

He silently hands us his letter. I flip it open and scan it, looking for anything that will ring alarm bells: legal implications, financial demands, exit negotiations. Nothing. It's a simple "I'm bowing out" kind of letter. He might be leaving us in the lurch, but he's a good guy and it would be out of character for him to make things ugly. He just wants a clean exit, a break. He's never been a fighter, and to be honest, our vicious lockdown-stressed spats were probably the final nail in the coffin.

I'm a bloody street dog. I hunger for fights. I go for the kill. I am energised by adversity. Sure, a peaceful, wholesome, loving life does sound appealing, but when there's a battle on the horizon, I flip a switch and become a rabid pit bull, exulting in my killer instinct and attack plans. Confrontation doesn't drain me; it delights me. From a certain perspective, thousands of years of humanity can be viewed as just a battle for dominance. This is our genetic inheritance. As Cersei Lannister told us in *Game of Thrones*: "I choose violence."

I'm the first to admit that some of my other character traits are that I tend to be extremely forceful, loud, overbearing and unrelenting in getting what I want. This means I can easily overpower people and drown out dissenting voices and conflicting opinions. This is a terrible trait for a founder, especially a young one – and, during the pandemic, I discover some ugly truths about my ego.

I often say, "I'm Alexandria Fucking Procter, and I always roll a six." But now the day has arrived when I roll a series of zeros. You'll probably say a die doesn't have a zero, but trust me, mine does. It has six faces of zeros.

After reading Michael's letter, Greg and I exchange a discreet look. Locking eyes even for a split-second is enough. We know that we are united now and always, and that we will continue to fight, to back each other, to overcome this, to manage it, and to make the company stronger. In these moments, there is no time for second-guessing. There can only be action. There can only be a commitment to move forward.

We soon find out where Michael is going.

Startups often attract a lot of attention. Ours did because it's thrilling that so much value can be created out of nothing, out of thin air, built by some crazy kids who were way too revved up on passion and dreams, and sure, probably a good dose of delusions that we'd overcome the odds and "save the world, baby".

So, crowds gather in the little startup ecosystems that churn out events, accelerators and incubators. There is also camaraderie among founders; we're cut from the same cloth and understand each other in a way most won't. In this little universe, there are unspoken rules and social contracts.

Truly gifted software developers are snapped up in a heartbeat and thus are rarer than compliments from a narcissist. While poaching isn't uncommon, it's considered taboo to poach from a friend's company – it's like having an affair with a friend's spouse. And, if you're an investor in a startup, it's unheard of to poach from your own portfolio company – it's like having an affair with your child's spouse. You undermine your own investment. It's crazy. You just don't do it. And, on top of all of that, to poach someone who is not only an employee but also an executive and cofounder is staggering.

It was a crazy time and people did crazy things, but I learnt a lot. In the end, I believe that the only way to live and build authentically is to engage with utter truth and openness. That is how one opens the door to true collaboration.

You just gotta listen to Bob Dylan telling us: "Don't think twice. It's alright." I believe one must truly wish the best for everyone on their journeys and then very quickly move on. Let it go and focus on the future.

CHAPTER 24

PERSPECTIVE

After we got over the shock of our CTO's resignation, Greg and I quickly come up with a plan for a smooth transition that will keep the team and our investors at ease. We also have to manage the public perception of his departure. We worry that it will seem like evidence of the company's impending death and that members of our team will bolt. What if we're unable to close the funding round that we desperately need because we are in sniffing distance of the end of our runway? I volunteer to take over the dev team as interim product leader. (It would be insanity to call myself the CTO, as I haven't touched the code base since we rebuilt in Django.) We decide to spin Michael's resignation as a "confidential personal issue" and not share details "out of respect for the parties involved".

Well, that plan fails.

When they hear the news, the dev team looks like someone has died. Without strong technical leadership, they feel adrift. We start losing team members almost weekly. Half of them bolt as soon as their notice periods are up. Now we're left with one full-time junior dev and one part-time dev. Neither has any context on half the code base.

Our platform isn't exactly rock solid, so when it crashes a few weeks later, we have no idea what happened, never mind how to fix it. I had naively shipped all product responsibility to Michael and left him to deal with the execution and implementation of my wild product ideas.

We do, however, see a faint light in all the darkness. In a tech startup, developers are always the most expensive employees. So, when we lose most of our team, our salary burden shrinks so drastically that it gives us much-needed breathing space. Our two remaining devs are also phenomenal. Having shouldered the burden of figuring out the entire platform pretty much overnight, they become some of the greatest assets on our team. The product becomes incredibly focused, clean and without clutter.

Once the business side of our CTO's departure has been taken care of, I let myself process the departure of my friend. We met a couple of years before, when I was running a small NGO focused on digital literacy in townships. He reached out to me in an out-of-the-blue Facebook DM, asking if he could join my team. Within three minutes of meeting, we were sharing our favourite Carl Sagan quotes, swapping book recommendations and listing secret swimming spots around the Peninsula. I had to wrench myself away to get back to work, and I was left buzzing for the next two days.

We started spending all our time together and soon

became more than friends. He was obsessed with startups. While I had fallen into the startup life and quite accidentally created something without really knowing what I'd done, he had been researching entrepreneurship for years, waiting for the right opportunity to jump in.

One evening, I arrived at his apartment after work. "I've already ordered for us. Food should be here in half an hour," he said. We both loved to eat.

"Look, I'd like to chat to you about something," he continued. "I want to join DigsConnect and be the CTO."

I didn't say anything at first. The thought had obviously crossed my mind.

I love building projects, and every time I meet someone new who is switched on, I immediately wonder how we can work together. I've learnt the hard way that this is not necessarily healthy. These days, I try (but often fail) to draw a clear divide between friends and colleagues. But back then, it seemed like a magical idea. I was the one building DigsConnect tech and product, and because I'm not exactly the pinnacle of engineering talent, our tech wasn't spectacular. We needed a CTO, but no highly skilled, highly talented, extraordinarily well-paid engineer was going to leave a cushy job to join a South African startup that couldn't pay them a salary. I knew Michael would be incredible in the role, but I also knew that it would put an end to our budding relationship. I hadn't wanted to make that choice, so I had pushed it out of my mind. But now he had asked me directly.

"Hmm. How do you imagine that would work? What are you looking for from this? And why?" I managed to sound in control. He gave his answers, and they were good.

"Cool, let me have a think and chat to Greg, and then get back to you?" I smiled at him, but in truth I felt a bit ill. The energy had shifted between us. The magic of our early, shy and naive connection was broken. We were no longer two people just sharing a journey of human connection. It had been stifled by the introduction of something transactional.

The next day, I went to visit one of my oldest friends from school. "Proc, I'm gonna be honest with you. Sounds like a bloody disaster. But whatever you decide to do, I'll back you."

When Greg, ever the grounded, sensible one, heard that Michael wanted in, he pulled me aside. In a way only he could cut through my bullshit, he said: "Proc, how do you really feel about this? Not what other people will think, not what he thinks, just how do you feel?"

"Weird," I admitted. I did feel weird about it. But nothing was more important to me than building the startup.

Once Michael started working with us, our sense of humour was our bridge and we laughed non-stop. We truly had a meeting of minds, and we spent countless nights together at the office after everyone had left, discussing Carl Sagan, SpaceX, startups, the future, philosophy, culture, effective altruism, science, culture and war. Then we'd race around Cape Town in his car or on his motorbike to some all-night cafe to feast at 3am, laughing hysterically at some exhausted, corny joke, always with feverish optimism for the future, or watch the city lights from the office windows. For a while, he was the person I felt closest to in the world. I really thought we would be building companies together forever.

It does no good to dwell on resentment. That's an easy statement to make, full of smug wisdom – as if it were that easy. Give me a break! Resentment is a warm bath to soak in, highly pleasurable as it slowly curdles your skin.

In my 30 years of life, I've had enough resentment and anger to fill the earth several times over, sometimes so much that I can't understand how it all fits in my body. It's strange, harbouring feelings of vengeance, because while you know they feel awful and prickly and thick like mucky tar, there's a sadistic pleasure in the pain you're inflicting on yourself by clinging to these emotions.

Finding peace is the journey of a lifetime. Whenever I think I've found the answers to grace and wisdom, I soon realise that I know absolutely nothing about either of these things. When I zoom into a particular problem, it feels massive, like the only thing that exists in the universe, the only injustice that's ever occurred. Then, when I manage to take a large step back, I see that our entire civilisation is just a layer of sediment on a rockface that a future generation or species or sentient AI will point at in a millennium or two and say, "Look on my works, ye mighty, and despair!" That's all we are. A layer of sediment.

On 14 February 1990, just before I was born, NASA's Voyager 1 took a photograph of the Earth at a distance of 6 billion kilometres from the sun. It's one of the most extraordinary photographs in the world, the famous "Pale Blue Dot". Witnessing it is a fundamental part of the human experience. That image, along with "Earthrise", is our one-way ticket to perspective. And perhaps it even shows us a sprinkling of peace and compassion.

Whenever I'm walking outside, I'll look up and remember with relish that just a mere hundred kilometres away lies the Kármán line – the outer boundary of the Earth, beyond which stretches infinity. It is indeed the world in a grain of sand … and infinity in the palm of your hand.

Once my mind has dwelt on these huge celestial places, the current inconveniences of life don't seem that bad after all. And, these days, when it comes to our former CTO, I've gained some much-needed perspective and peace.

But back in 2021, time ticks away over the following months and the country remains in lockdown. Another Covid wave arrives, and videos of chaos and death and overcrowded hospitals flood social media. A feeling of powerless panic seeps through the deserted streets just outside my apartment's windows. It's deathly still; no movement, no money, no cars, just a silent fear that spreads across our world, just curtains in street-side windows flicked open by suspicious neighbours. And all the while our runway shortens and our prospects diminish.

CHAPTER 25

SICK ... AND TIRED

"This is the way the world ends, not with a bang but a whimper." – *The Hollow Men*, T.S. Eliot

I've never thought of myself as an anxious person, and until 2020–21, the word "anxiety" didn't really exist in my world. So, in the second year of the pandemic and year two of trying to keep DigsConnect alive in a world under lockdown, in a country where campuses are shut, trying to figure out how the hell we're going to meet payroll, month after month, wondering whether the very core of the business is still viable, I start to feel constant dread but I don't even have a word for it. It's just a feeling that the floor is about to fall away at any moment, that the sky is collapsing, that there is some impending doom around the corner and that I am living on borrowed time.

I keep seeing disasters everywhere. Even though I have a pilot's licence and have been in full training for my full PPL (private pilot's licence) at Stellenbosch Flying Club, flying Cessna 152s, Jabberwockys and Pipers, I am now terrified of flying. The girl who once spent nearly every day in the ocean is now terrified of water. Small, once-manageable things now freak me out. One day, my car gets a flat tyre while I'm driving. Whatever, right? Just a flat tyre. But when I get out and see the deflated rubber, knowing that I'm going to miss my meetings, I collapse. I just can't take it anymore. I start weeping at the side of the road.

Usually, I would just hail an Uber, get on with my day and call a mate to help me change the tyre. But now I am sobbing in a heap at the side of the road. I feel beyond exhausted.

I've also never been a sickly person. I can probably count on one hand the number of times I've been seriously unwell in my life, but now I'm constantly getting colds and the flu. I've had a consistent headache for about six weeks, and I'm living on paracetamol. I'm not a sleep-driven person – usually five hours a night will suffice – but during this time, I am so exhausted by 5pm that most days end with me crying.

I find myself crawling into bed by 6pm or just falling into a heap on the cold tiles, as every part of me feels drained beyond belief. There is nothing left. The tank is empty. I sleep for 12-hour stretches and wake up consumed with unshakable dread. I struggle to psych myself up, to jump onto the morning standup video call with the team to spread positivity and love. Those 20-minute calls drain me so completely that as soon as I hang up, I lie on the floor in whatever sunny patch I can find in my apartment and stare at the white ceiling.

I've known for a long time that I've almost certainly got

ADHD. For my whole life, I've been a terror to teachers and everyone around me due to explosive, overwhelming energy, bouncing off my seat, speaking too loudly and too fast, racing around and having this nuclear-reactor supernova constantly exploding inside me. All that energy now seems to have disappeared. It feels like I'm at the bottom of the barrel, at the end of the road. Everything inside me that made me who I am feels used up. I'm terrified that it isn't coming back.

I don't know how I am going to get up off the floor. I'm depleted. Yet, I also know that so much is resting on me at DigsConnect. I'm still the one who has to figure it all out. People are depending on me. Their livelihoods weigh heavily on me. Most of them have dependants, and there's a lot of other people's money riding on my ability to perform. And not just to perform – to excel.

Stress can manifest in many ways. One of the ways it hits me during Covid is that I stop menstruating. I've always been super-regular and pretty healthy. I don't drink much alcohol, except on rare occasions. I don't smoke. I hardly ever go to bars. I've been to a club maybe twice in my life (and hated it both times). I exercise daily.

Yes, I have somewhat of an addiction to fresh *pain au chocolat* from Parisian Boulangeries, or Lindt bunnies at Easter, but that's mostly under control (sort of). However, the body keeps the score, and the series of hard blows during the pandemic has begun to take root. In a bid to conserve cash at the company, Greg and I continue to slash our salaries until I can't afford to pay rent and have to borrow money with no idea how I am going to pay it back. Welcome to debt, Alexandria.

I have never faced personal financial uncertainty before. It is a humbling lesson. It's a gargantuan privilege not to be in debt, and something I hadn't even noticed until I wasn't able to afford paying rent. Suddenly, the world feels a lot scarier. Rent, groceries, medical aid, petrol, Wi-Fi, cellphone data, taxes, subscriptions – all have to be paid.

My beloved apartment, my home, my piles and piles of books, my jungle of indoor plants, my art and my eclectic assortment of furniture that I found and that found me at kooky little antique fairs around the country are now just price tags that can help me get by for a couple of weeks. It's a peculiarly horrible feeling to watch strangers come into your home, size up your beloved things and offer you half their worth – which you accept in your desperation before you watch them being carted off. It's just stuff, right? Well, that's a lie, because I loved that stuff. It made me feel cosy; it made me feel at home.

My apartment looks like it has been violated. Strange energies have entered and familiar ones have left. It feels like my beautiful way of life is disappearing, like dead birds are falling from the sky around me and I am solely to blame.

Now I eat dinner alone, sitting on my kitchen counter or on the floor, the plate resting on my cold, pale knees. I become opaque. I'm alone because I simply have no words to say to anyone. I'm often awake before dawn because of my ridiculously early bedtimes. Sitting on the white windowsill, watching as the sky changes colour, does not bring peace. The irony is that I'm the founder and CEO of what is essentially a housing platform. I provide homes for a living, and now it feels like I'm about to be homeless.

Throughout this time, I'm being reminded of the importance of our task in the most visceral of ways.

A home is more than four walls and a roof. A home is a sense of safety, security, comfort and peace. It is a sanctuary. It is the foundation that we need for every other aspect of our lives to work. It all starts with having a place to call "home". For aeons, humans have gathered in safe spaces with their possessions to protect their vulnerabilities. This is what DigsConnect is all about. And this is what is being plucked from me, minute by minute, hour by hour, as I scrape by and borrow fistfuls of cash for day-to-day living.

Then a disgruntled ex-employee decides to take us to the South African labour court for wrongful dismissal. As CEO, I need to handle this.

The dismissal had been entirely fair, and our labour lawyer agreed. He also added that South African labour law favoured the employee: no matter how legal, ethical or fair the dismissal was, we could lose.

"We don't have any money!" I tell him.

"Then you, as director and CEO, will be liable."

On our court date, I negotiate a settlement that we can afford and the case is dismissed, but the whole experience is not a pleasant one.

My period is a no-show that month and is missing in action the following one too. The medical term for "no period" is amenorrhoea. Most doctors don't take it all that seriously. They shrug you off and leave you to do your own googling and panicking. You try to explain that you've never been late in your life. You say, "Yes, I'm certain I'm not pregnant. Aren't there any blood tests I can do?" They usually say, "Wait."

Then the new investors with whom we are in due diligence call to say they're pulling out of the deal. The term sheet was already out but hadn't been signed. There is too much market uncertainty, they say. What they mean is, "You're fucked, and we're out."

Still no period.

After another month has gone by, I make an appointment with my gynaecologist. A week later, I get a voicemail inbox from him, saying that I need to call him back urgently. I am terrified. It turns out the pap smear results show some dodgy cells in my cervix that the gynae is concerned about.

A few weeks later, I am wheeled into the operating theatre. The gynaecologist is relaxed about the whole situation. I get local anaesthetic (so that I can continue to be productive that afternoon) and I happily chat to the nurses in the room throughout the procedure.

"All done! See, easy-peasy!" he says to me. He then asks if I want to see what was cut out. "Yeah sure!" I answer, curious as always. He holds up the part of my cervix wall that has been removed.

It's not often that moments suddenly and irrevocably change you – where there's a sudden paradigm shift. Usually change, if it happens at all, is gradual. But this moment fundamentally changes me. I remember the shock, a tectonic shift in my being, at seeing a part of my body cut out and held up by metal forceps, covered in my blood. I feel a bit nauseous, and I do what I always do when I feel discomfort: I laugh.

Back home, minus a part of my cervix, I pop a couple of painkillers and dive back into DigsConnect.

Life moves on. The next month, still no period. The

following month, still nothing. Another month goes by –
no period.

Around the same time, I also start getting intense
headaches. They are piercing and pervasive, and they last
for days. I go for an MRI to try to find out what the hell
is happening. The images that come back from the scan
completely mesmerise me. The photos of each tiny layer of
my brain flick past like a video, and I watch as my brain
forms before my eyes.

That's my brain! That's it. That's me! That's me, Alexandria.

I can literally *see* my sense of humour, my personality.
My skull holds my perception of existence, my entire
universe. My comprehension of the existence of others, of
pain. My ideas, my plans for the future of humanity. The
victories and the heartaches and my sense of time passing,
the colours I see and the textures I feel, all that I don't see
or feel, and all my biases and everything I'll be or never
be. All zooming around on little electrical currents in that
grey matter.

Homo sapiens: hundreds of millions of years of evolution
to create one of the most complex and beautiful structures
in the known universe – the human brain, the human
consciousness.

Seeing my brain leaves me feeling strangely happy in
a grateful kind of way. I realise that the mistake I made
was to see all the tasks ahead of me as a burden. I was
resentful of everything. Work had become a toil. It was
imprisonment. I disliked it, so it disliked me right back. I
now see how ridiculous that was. Because here's the thing:
the challenge is not the burden; *the challenge is the gift.*

What other life could I be leading? What else could I

possibly do with this crazy brain of mine, this explosive life of mine? What else if not burn, burn, burn, explode and come alive again? What the hell else? What is this body, this brain, this life for if not to give it everything you've got?

How many years of life do I have left? I know the end of this movie already. It isn't like there is an escape hatch. It's coming for all of us. It ends the same way no matter what I do. So why not give it another shot?

My period comes back about six months later. The headaches, the fatigue, the anxiety and the amenorrhoea were all symptoms of major burnout.

CHAPTER 26

YOU CAN'T EAT THE FREEDOM CHARTER

By the end of 2021, South Africa is still firmly under Level 3 lockdown, and most university classes are happening remotely. There is mounting pressure on the government to let students return to campus. A massive hurdle is South Africa's vast inequality. *Cry, the beloved country!* We're straddling two worlds. One includes moneyed Johannesburg and Cape Town, tech hubs and high finance, old money and new wealth – the glorious, delirious passion of Africa rising. And then, a couple of hundred metres down the road, there is another world of endless miles of shacks and townships and poverty and hopelessness, of millions of forgotten people.

In the early 1950s, the leaders of the African National Congress spent years organising and campaigning, travelling apartheid South Africa from urban township to rural village, remote farm to ramble-down homesteads, as they sought to establish a unified vision for a democratic and non-racial South Africa. The result was the Freedom Charter, which was adopted on 26 June 1955 at a gathering of the Congress of the People, a coalition of the ANC, the South African Indian Congress, the Coloured People's Congress and the South African Congress of Trade Unions.

"We, the People of South Africa, declare for all our country and the world to know: that South Africa belongs to all who live in it, black and white, and that no government can justly claim authority unless it is based on the will of all the people…"

The creation of the Freedom Charter led to the arrest of 156 activists, including Nelson Mandela, in 1956. They were charged with high treason for daring to say that the country belonged to all who lived in it, that its resources should be shared among its people, that all discriminatory laws should be abolished and that a democratic government should govern South Africa.

The charter formed the basis of the South African constitution that was adopted when we became a democracy in 1994. Its words remain powerful and true. But more than that, it is a symbol of hope and inspiration for all who seek a more just and equitable world. It galvanises us to be better, to try harder, to remember the dream of a promised land and our commitment to getting there.

But for those who are starving, the Freedom Charter cannot be transformed into a few slices of bread and fed to children with extended bellies.

The huge wealth gap in our country feels like a giant rift in the land itself. There are rural towns and villages with roads reduced to rubble from all the potholes that have never been fixed by corrupt municipal officials. We straddle these two worlds every day. And, by 2022, the divide has been even more brutally exacerbated by the two-year lockdown.

Studying from home might be great if you're privileged and wealthy, with access to a consistent source of electricity and Wi-Fi and online tutors that your parents can afford. If, on the other hand, you are one of the 690 000 government-funded students whose total family income is below R250 000 a year (about $13 000–$15 000), it's unlikely that you'll have your own laptop, let alone your own room in which to study. Chances are you will be inundated with crucial family chores and responsibilities. Any government money that comes to you for learning will find its way to more urgent matters, like food for your hungry siblings.

During the two years of lockdown-enforced online learning, failure rates soar – as do mental health issues. The mounting pressure from an already quasi-militant student body means that universities will have to return to on-campus lessons in 2022. But this is the insane time of Covid, where nothing is certain and the South African government still has sweeping authority over our liberties and rights through its state-of-disaster legislation.

At DigsConnect, we've always focused on the challenges faced by underprivileged students in South Africa. We are all too aware of the harsh reality. It has sometimes literally knocked on our doors, like the time a student took a 12-hour bus trip across the country and didn't know where else to go. He wound up at DigsConnect HQ with all his belongings in a tog bag and a university acceptance letter in hand. I remember how shocked we were the first time this happened. Eventually, we lost count of how often it occurred. I just grew angrier at the universities and the government, so lost in their own indifference that they had literally no plans for these students. One by one, we found these students homes with our listed landlords who took them in on good faith until the government payouts arrived (usually at least four months late).

The stats are depressing. Only one in three university students in South Africa will graduate. Among the multitudes of underprivileged students, this number is even lower. Poverty cycles are vicious, and the rip current is strong. The odds that these students must overcome are staggering, but the country depends on them breaking out of poverty through education. Indeed, I would say that our entire viability as a country and a functioning democracy depends on migrating the bulk of the population from poverty to the middle class. A nation is not won only once; 1994 was just the first step along a long road for those still shackled by poverty. A nation must be won every day, every time the disenfranchised become empowered, lest our complacent belief in our constitution (which sometimes feels somewhat devoid of reality) makes us forget what the dream of progress can look like, smell like, feel like.

Without property, without sustainable livelihoods, with no sense of security, with no sense of ownership of the homes and neighbourhoods where people live, there is a fundamental breakdown of community and society, and there can be no nation-building. You cannot build a country with a nation of desperate, hungry and property-less citizens. Furthermore, citizens robbed of an education cannot hold their leaders to account, so corruption runs rampant. A functioning education system, ownership of property and a large tax base are fundamental ingredients of a secure democracy. Instead, we see a tax base that is shrinking, a public education system that is crumbling and a growing property-less population who feel no ownership of their country and thus are understandably prone to violent protests to vent their unanswered rage at unrealised promises.

We need these students from underprivileged backgrounds to get their education, graduate, get jobs, join the workforce, contribute to the tax base and increase the circulation of money, trade, financial transactions and mercantile relationships in our country. Getting this right is the only way that South Africa can be saved, if we want to remain a free, market-based democracy.

Having worked on the frontlines and butted heads with the highly flawed system, we decided to publish a report on the data we had collected, combined with our experiences in the sector in 2020 when we were in deep lockdown and the critical issues became starkly evident. In our report, we elaborated on the opportunities and solutions that we saw in fixing this by working with all the stakeholders in the space – the government, NGOs, corporates and universities.

This report would be picked up by the World Bank's International Development Association. I would subsequently be interviewed by their team and they would go on to publish their own extensive market analysis on how we at DigsConnect were growing the student housing sector.

CHAPTER 27

NEVER LET A GOOD CRISIS GO TO WASTE

What's driving me crazy is that I know that everything will start to work if only the country can just come out of lockdown. As long as there is property and there are landlords, there will be a need for tenants. As long as there are people who bloody well live somewhere, we have a business. Furthermore, this model worked for all our competitors offshore ... and that's when it hits me.

Offshore!

The consensus at the time is that South African startups should not, under any circumstances, attempt to launch offshore, not until they've made several millions, locally, in revenue to validate the model. They should ideally be profitable and have insider market knowledge, networks and substantial offshore investors lined up, or better yet, be in a position where they've bought an offshore competitor.

After having cut every cost humanly possible (including my and Greg's salaries to the bare minimum, just to cover our residential rent), we can hardly keep our servers running, never mind buy or even compete with an offshore competitor. But by late 2021, while South Africa is still in this seemingly endless lockdown, there is now a sliver of hope: other countries in the world have started opening up. By August 2021, northern Europe, notably in the same time zone as us, has ended all lockdowns.

In my research into picking the best market for DigsConnect, one name has kept popping up: Student.com. They were the first global name – and are now the biggest – in student housing. They are well-funded and thoroughly entrenched in all the markets that we have our eyes on. Going head to head with them will be tough, especially considering that we literally have no money.

Sometimes the odds are so stacked against you that the situation enters the realm of the absurd. While Student.com is the biggest competitor, they are by no means the only competitor. If we can just keep extending our runway, we will be going head to head with several international direct competitors and a whole host of local players who all understand local contexts far better than we do.

When we graph out the restraining factors, we are left with areas in between the lines of possibility, where solutions can be found. But we also face a multitude of obstacles that render the situation near-impossible: no money, many well-funded competitors, and no international travel or on-the-ground brand building due to Covid-related travel restrictions. We are also a tiny group of exhausted founders running a small team with low morale. But sometimes the more restrictions you face, the more creative you have to be. Sometimes a comfy blank canvas is the innovator's worst enemy.

As Day Zero Cash draws closer, I begin to experience sudden intense surges of energy. One day, as I am driving through Green Point, my mind hits upon the memory of a person. I swerve wildly across the road into a side street in De Waterkant and come to a halt on a red line. I grab my bag from the backseat and rip out my phone.

I've just remembered that a year or two ago, I gave a talk at a tech event. Afterwards, one of the audience members approached me. Quite a few people had wanted to talk to me after the event, and while I couldn't recall our exact conversation, I remember this guy who had told me that he was family friends with one of the founders of Student.com. I remember giving him my email address and telling him to chase me up for a coffee. But I had also lost control of my inbox months ago (as I type these words, I'm on 3 768 unread emails), and had subsequently lost track of emails in the deluge. Inbox zero is but a pipe dream for me.

"What was his name?" I shout aloud in the car, scrolling and scrolling through emails on my phone. I decide to search my calendar for the event. I find it and take note of the date. His email would surely have been sent shortly after? I filter my emails to that week and about 600 pop up. Okay, that is a non-starter. I try a few keywords and – BANG BOOM CRASH POW WOW BINGO WINNER-WINNER CHICKEN DINNER LUCKY NUMBER ONE! There it is! In my inbox. Still unread!

Hardly breathing, I open the email. At the bottom is his phone number. It feels as if a huge helium balloon is being blown up inside my chest, growing bigger and bigger, lifting me off the ground, defying gravity. At the same time, I'm terrified by the possibility that it could pop or explode at any second and I'll come crashing down into a heap of failed dreams and disappointment. But above all else, there's a feeling of the beautiful, devastatingly gorgeous human spirit of hope, of the middle finger to disillusionment, the revolutionary fist standing before the tanks of oppression, against all odds, the oh-my-God-this-might-work, this-might-actually-fucking-work! Holy shit!

Fingers shaking, I dial his number. It goes straight to voicemail. I save his contact and quickly open WhatsApp. His contact appears with a profile picture. Yes – that's him. I remember his face now. I call from WhatsApp. It rings. Once, twice, three times, four times – nausea slowly rising in the back of my throat – and then he answers.

"George!" I scream. Crikey, I can't even imagine what my voice must have sounded like. Imagine getting a phone call out of the blue from someone who gave a talk more than a year ago and who then ignored your email but who's now screeching like a beer-soaked, blood-thirsty audience member at a Texan monster-truck rally.

"George! How the bloody hell are you? It's Alexandria Procter from DigsConnect!"

Silence.

"Alexandria? Oh wow! This is unexpected. How are you?"

Relief. He seems genuinely happy to be speaking to me. "So sorry for the WhatsApp call. I tried to call you normally but the phone was engaged!"

"Yeah, I've moved to Berlin, and I have a German number now. I was going to update my WhatsApp number to my German number today, so you caught me just in time!"

My heart rate hits an all-time high. (I swear to God

the music from *Inception* was playing somewhere in the background.)

Now, the thing about being desperate is that you cannot under any circumstances let on that you're a desperado. People can smell desperation a mile off, and nothing makes them run away faster. It's an instinctual reaction to flee the sinking ship. Desperate = flee. Even though some people might say, "I'll always be there for you, come rain or shine, no matter what," desperation has a way of making phone calls and doorbells go unanswered. So, you have to mask it, play it cool, be nonchalant and irreverent.

"Yeah, everything's great." (The only person I have been able to truly share my desperation with is Greg, and it's one of the reasons why our bond is so unshakable. That kind of trust and loyalty runs deep.)

Channelling my most upbeat and nonchalant voice, without sounding at all needy despite never having been more desperate in my entire life, I casually ask George if he still knows that person at Student.com that he told me about all those months ago. He does.

"Ah, cool man, cool … who is it?" I ask, trying to keep my tone even, fully expecting it to be some finance bro or intern.

"It's Luke Nolan, the founder and CEO. I'll send you his number now."

Wait! What?!

You know those dreams where you're falling? The feeling of the floor of your stomach just evaporating, free-fall, terror, impending doom? That's how I have been feeling every day for the past few months. And now, suddenly, in a split-second, it feels like I have grown wings. It's the feeling of a lifeline. It's the feeling of a second chance in an unfair world. It's the feeling of being carried to your bed at night by your dad after you've fallen asleep in front of the TV while watching your favourite cartoon next to your brother. It's the feeling of reaching the shore after you've just been dunked by a huge tidal wave.

I say goodbye to George and make a mental note to owe him the biggest favour possible, as soon as I can. A few seconds later, my phone beeps. George has sent Luke's number. I feel like falling to the ground and smooching the pavement. Something about this moment feels huge. I can't really say what it is. I mean, by this point I've met hundreds of fancy CEOs, investors and politicians, but something about this feels … dare I say … destined?

I get out of my car, good old trusty Angela Merkel, and pace up and down the street, mentally composing the perfect message. After a couple of seconds, I have it. I sit on the pavement and my thumbs get to work. Being a founder means perfecting your pitch. When you're trying to get a moment with someone who's undoubtedly very busy, you have to prove instantly that you're worthy of their attention. It must be short but deeply impactful. I type out a punchy message, read through it twice to check for typos, select the perfect emojis to convey a sense of my personality, take a huge intake of breath and hit "Send".

As soon as it's gone, I jump up and down on the pavement like a sped-up Jane Fonda workout video. I do a couple of star jumps and sprint to the end of the road and back. The hipsters lounging around the array of trendy Cape Town coffee shops *skeef* me out, but the build-up of tension at this point is so intense that I have to release it.

I call Greg and give him the rundown. He has tight control of his emotions – or maybe he's also so emotionally dead after all the strain that he no longer allows himself to get excited about anything. Without a hint of exhilaration, he simply says: "It sounds like a good lead. Let's see what happens, Proc."

I jog a couple more loops around the block, leaping up every now and then to hit a road sign and hear the metallic CLANG!, high-fiving the car guards, biting my fists, my mind running like mad. I get back into my car and, just as I'm about to drive home, my phone pings.

"Hey, Alexandria! Thanks for reaching out, and well done on all the success to date! Sure, a call sounds interesting. Let's set it up. Luke."

Three weeks later, lockdown travel restrictions have been lifted. On 24 September, Greg and I are on a flight to Dubai to meet the execs of Student.com. They have been keen to launch in Africa for a couple of years, but they've been cautious to take the plunge without insider market access. Our market expertise, traction and brand equity appear to make us interesting to them.

We have arranged to meet up with them at a café, a Mexican joint called Senor Pico, on the Palm Jumeirah. It has a spectacular view of Dubai. Greg and I arrive early. It is a gorgeous evening with a warm desert breeze. Coming from tiny Port Elizabeth in the rugged, rural Eastern Cape, Dubai feels like another planet. Colossal structures of iron, concrete and glass rise up hundreds of metres and set the sky ablaze with twinkling lights, all reflecting on the ocean, dotted with superyachts.

The Student.com team arrives and immediately orders a round of margaritas. With shouts of "Cheers!" and clinking glasses, the seeds are sown for an epic partnership. We are in for a hell of a night.

A few days later, we sign a partnership deal with the biggest student housing group in the world that sees DigsConnect.com listing 1.3 million beds worldwide and launching globally!

The news of the deal hits the international media and, in particular, lands with a bang in South Africa, where good news has become rare.

On 20 October 2021, the front page of the *Business Insider* is a photograph of Luke, Greg and me. The headline is: "Never let a good crisis go to waste, says DigsConnect. com CEO as she inks global deal".

Based on the back of this massive door that has opened for us, we now secure an angel investment from the CEO of one of South Africa's largest banks that will cover our costs and get us to January 2022, when our South African busy season will start – should the lockdown end and the universities return to business as usual. If we have a profitable South African season, the revenue will bolster a good enough valuation to raise capital for a global launch, defending the business against future regional chaos. We know that January will be tough, but we have suddenly been given enough breathing room to survive until then. Our runway has leapt forward by a couple more months, and we are back in the ring, swinging.

Shortly after Greg and I return to Cape Town from the

Student.com meetings in Dubai, we receive a call from an American charity organisation that has been doing work in the student accommodation space. We had first met them in 2019, and over the many months of lockdown, we had stayed in touch.

Our report on the state of student accommodation, which I mentioned in the previous chapter, has come to their attention. They want to support our work and further our impact in helping disadvantaged students find accommodation. Their research has shown a clear link between academic success and secure housing amongst financially challenged students. After a due diligence process, we get the nod from their parent organisation in Austin, Texas and they decide to give us a grant to support our work.

After the call with this organisation, Greg closes his laptop slowly and turns to face me. I am already staring at him. We have literally two days before the end of the month when our team's salaries are due and the debit orders will go off the company account. Only a couple of weeks ago, we would not have been able to afford any of these payments. Between these three deals, we suddenly have enough in the bank for at least the next six months into 2022. There are no words.

The past 24 months and everything that has happened are with us in the room: what we have lost, what we have sacrificed and now, finally, what we have gained.

Slowly, we start to laugh. It turns into manic hysteria.

"Dude, holy shit," I try to speak. "I – I – oh my God. What?!"

"Let's go, then!" Greg yells, and we jump up and run

like two madmen down the street, leaping and hugging each other and laughing. Oh my God, oh my God! It's like we're being reborn. A vice-like grip slowly releases from my chest. I can feel the sun on my face again. It's summer in South Africa, and the warmth spreads through my lungs and feels like doors that have been opened in an old, abandoned house.

That afternoon, we run down to our favourite beachside cafe and work our way through a bottle of champagne and a couple of margaritas. Because, homies, we are ALIVE!

The next day, there is no time for further celebrations. We have been given a chance in a million, and now we have to run with it. Our busy season is approaching. We have modelled our cashflow and sales projections to a tee, week by week; now we have to hit them to reach the valuation we need for a subsequent round.

The first step is to get the team on board. In its early days, a startup is nothing without the people who are building it. Established businesses have a degree of inertia that carry them forward, but startups run on the lifeblood of the team. If the blood supply dries up, the startup dies. Especially when a black-swan event like the pandemic occurs and the market goes into freefall.

CHAPTER 28

BRUTAL PANDEMIC LESSONS

As much as the Covid lockdown is hardcore, in hindsight it is possibly the best thing that could happen to DigsConnect and to me as a founder. It's like an MBA in entrepreneurship – on steroids. It is sink-or-swim incarnate. It's a lifetime of lessons squeezed into an hour, and every minute we endure what is being shoved down our throats. We try to not choke.

I hate blaming circumstances for whatever happens. I refuse to. As a conscious adult human being, I am not someone who wrestles with excuses. I am alive and I have a brain. I believe these are the core prerequisites for succeeding and doing good in the world. Furthermore, fate's roll of the dice has allowed me to be born into a life of privilege: for the past three decades, I have been educated, fed and housed. I am alive in the 21st century at a time where I have my human rights enshrined. I have access, via the internet, to the collected knowledge of our entire species and multiple civilisations, past and present, through a device in my pocket that is available to me 24/7.

There are no excuses. Blaming our circumstances doesn't just make us bad losers. It also does something far worse: it stunts our entire being, our creativity, and kills off our most magnificent ideas. So, when this virus arrives in town and we go into lockdown, I make a concerted effort to not let it mess with our plans, to not be the victim.

At DigsConnect, we react fast to the change of circumstance and show exceptionally good governance, but none of us have any idea how long the lockdown will last. We all know what happens next. Universities shut down. Students are forced to stay off campus. Lectures go online, and tenants cancel leases. The economy nose-dives, and despite my deeply held views on not becoming a victim of circumstance, there are times when rampant panic replaces hope.

Despite our very best efforts to manage the situation, we, like many other businesses around the world, are trapped in a nightmare. It's extremely disorientating. We were on a huge crest of success, and now we are watching our business being decimated by a tidal wave. We cut salaries while the end of our runway looms large and menacingly.

Eventually, we have just 20 days of runway left before the company will have to shut its doors, Greg and I sit in the boardroom, clutching ourselves, pacing around and throwing idea after idea at each other before shredding them as unfeasible. But while the world is collapsing all around us, some standout lessons start to take shape.

The crisis tests my abilities in every possible way and, most importantly, makes me transform the "idea" of *building* a startup into actually *doing* it. I realise that all the lofty things that people talk about, tweet about or post about on Instagram are nothing close to reality.

Covid exposed all the holes in our business. DigsConnect had been built in an entirely different, pre-Covid era. This "grow at all costs" mentality was now being shown to be unsustainable. While we had inadvertently stumbled upon something that had worked in the sense that students and landlords loved it, and it had spread like wildfire, we had no idea how to monetise it in the early days.

The goals weren't wrong per se, but they were not in the right order. Marketing can only be built on a solid product, which in turn can be built only on a solid business model. The model needs to work first and foremost. At the very least, you need to make enough money to cover your burn so that your runway doesn't spell death for your company. And so I am forced to realise during the Covid crisis that our business model and product need to pivot – massively.

When you've been on a high like we were pre-Covid, coming back down to earth feels rough. After we analyse the key performance indicators and do some basic modelling, it becomes clear that our "growth over profitability" model and our *laissez-faire* approach to breaking even (we have generated millions by this point, but we have spent far, far more) isn't going to be sustainable. Analysis of the user experience and feature-funnel conversion rate also shows a less-than-desirable and unfocused product. The business model must change radically.

Our rocket ship needs a new direction, and at our burn rate, it needs a new one fast. Telling our team, a group of people committed to one path, that they have to change tack isn't easy, especially during a pandemic when business has all but died. The phrase "going backwards" is thrown at me a lot; try as I might to navigate it, there is an upwelling of resentment among the team members, aimed at me. While we have managed our budget well enough to not need to retrench staff during the Covid-induced economic tailspin and university closures, we're unable to pay bonuses or meet annual salary increases, which doesn't help with morale.

But the simple truth is that you cannot bite off more than you can chew. Sure, you can eat an elephant, but you can only do it one bite at a time. This startup grew insanely over the first two years, with user and bed stock numbers at ridiculous levels. We had tens of millions of rand worth of leases moving through our platform, and we were generating real value in the broader scheme of things as well as trying damn hard to fulfil our social mandate of "no student should ever be homeless".

However, some fundamental product flaws meant that I had no idea how the company could capture a percentage of the value generated. Even worse, I had no idea how to ensure consistent quality in the delivery of our services and products to users as we scaled. There is a very real security risk in South Africa, and as user numbers swelled, Greg and I became increasingly paranoid about bad faith actors who could be populating our platform. The only way I could sum up my change in thinking when I insisted on a pivot was: "Sometimes, in order to be big, you first have to be small."

I want to feel in control again of the value offering, of this massive sprawling creature that has begun generating more angst than assistance. I need resources to do that, so it becomes clear to me that the first step is to fully monetise the platform. Our users are used to it being free – but I have learnt a fundamental truth: nothing is free. And when something seems too good to be true, it usually is. Either you're the product (like in the case of Facebook, where you're monetised as a user) or someone else is taking the financial hit somewhere along the value chain. At DigsConnect, we are taking the hit – and it's unsustainable. A service is being provided, and it needs compensation.

Telling users that they have to start paying for what they've been getting for free leads to exactly what I'd expected: a massive kick to the balls and an exodus from our site that has until then been experiencing explosive growth. Switching to fully monetised means that product flaws are suddenly under the spotlight. When you're paying for something, the small things that annoyed you when it was still free are no longer minor; now they're reasons to fume and complain.

As the interim CTO, I have to fix the problems fast while still pivoting the product to adjust to our new model.

While the effects of this extreme change are devastating at first, it is the only way forward: to create a long-term sustainable business that will cover its burn first and foremost (that is, show real, revenue-based traction, not just hype traction) and be something of real value that can then be upscaled to sustain itself.

The pandemic forces us to create more checks and balances with metrics against which to assess our performance, and I find mentors to call me out on fallacious thinking. I learn so much.

It wasn't only the relationship between Greg and me that strengthened during the pandemic stresses. We discovered just how fortunate we had been in finding our incredible investors. They came through for us with resources, opportunities, networks and support during that extremely tricky time. They were and still are always in our corner. They taught me so much, and continue to do so, about what a good business is, about making deals, about the importance of reputation and networking, and about how money can be made in this bizarre, hyper-connected world of transactions and adults and finance and markets. What's more, they walked alongside us with humour and made the ride a hell of a fun journey. I often think about how hard it must have been for them to not give up on us.

To be brutally honest, things get really scary at one point. The runway is so bad that I can't even admit it to my mentor. I start liquidating every asset I own to pour money into the company. I sell my personal belongings (clothing, jewellery, furniture).

By this stage, we have been forced to give up our office and sell off every moveable asset: desks, the fridge, the microwave, the couch, even our office plants. We're a real group of ragamuffins by now. But we stick together, working at coffee shops or on Greg's couch while Dylan feeds us snacks, laughing through it, caffeinating through it, never letting go of the dream.

By the time we sign the deals with Student.com, the angel investor and the US charity organisation at the end of 2021, it feels like we have just walked out of the desert into an oasis. Our team is a fraction of its original size. After our CTO left, most of the development team jumped ship in the vacuum of strong technical leadership. We've also bled team members from ops because we could not increase salaries during lockdown. So, in the last months of 2021, there are only six of us left on Team DigsConnect: me, Greg, one full-time back-end dev, one part-time front-end dev and two support members who double up as sales staff while also doing invoicing and ops.

When the lockdowns end, the world that we once were so sure of, with all its flaws and beauty, is unrecognisable. Many housing companies and other businesses have been crushed, but DigsConnect has survived only by the closest shave of the metaphorical ball sack.

We emerge scarred but forever transformed after our fight with death itself. Initially, our victory is tenuous but our relentless work on our partnerships locally and abroad will result in us regaining our seat as the continent's largest student accommodation marketplace, except this time we are doing it with unit economics that make financial sense. We even hire a product manager from one of our competitors during their liquidation. It's brutal, but while I learn a lot about kindness and compassion, I also learn that it's a dog-eat-dog world out there, kiddos.

CHAPTER 29

POLITICS & THE NYDA

The year 2021 has been by far the hardest of my life. On 1 December 2021 at around 10pm, as I'm sitting at my laptop going through our product pipeline for December, my phone rings. Unknown number. At first, I don't answer because a call at 10pm on a Wednesday night seems suspicious. The phone rings again. Frustrated and ready to be rude, I answer, expecting an AI voice trying to sell me car insurance.

"Alexandria Procter?"

"Hi, yes, speaking. Can I help you?"

"This is Sipho, special advisor to His Excellency President Cyril Ramaphosa."

I almost drop the phone but quickly pull myself together.

"Hi! How are you?"

"Well, thank you. Miss Procter, the president has appointed you to be a director of the National Youth Development Agency of South Africa. It's a three-year term, starting immediately."

Many months earlier, I received a call from a friend whom I had served with on my local ward council in my spare time, after I'd been elected as the women's representative for ward 59. (The ward council oversees governance at the level of a collection of suburbs and city councillors, and then reports to the mayor and so on up. It doesn't get more grassroots than councillors, and it's a great place to spend time if you have a passion for public governance and how communities organise themselves.) I had started my Libraries for Entrepreneurship project in the Cape Flats while on the ward council, and one of the other councillors had been impressed by the project and suggested that my name be put forward for the new NYDA board.

The process was gruelling. After submitting an extensive application form and motivation essay, the State Security Agency started running background checks. My name was then included on the first shortlist. The candidates were given time slots to be grilled in Parliament on live national television by the subcommittee responsible for youth affairs and overseeing the NYDA's activities. (This video is still on YouTube if you're curious to see how this author presented herself.)

Thereafter, the parliamentary committee put forward the final list of recommended names to the president so he could choose seven directors.

Months had passed since my parliamentary interview, and I had been so consumed by keeping Digs alive during the final months of 2021 that I'd almost completely forgotten about the NYDA thing. Now, as I listen to the voice on the other end of the line, my phone slightly sweaty against my cheek, my heart gallops wildly.

"Yes, of course, excellent. Thank you." I keep control of my voice.

"I'll email you more information now, Miss Procter, along with your appointment letter. Your presence is required in Pretoria immediately for your board induction and training. Your travel details and official passport will be sent to you shortly. Good night."

The phone goes dead. I stare at it for a second and then call Greg. After a couple of rings, he answers sleepily. (Greg always goes to bed at about 9.30pm.)

"Greg! Greg, holy shit! I just got appointed to the board of the NYDA! Dude, I'm meeting the president in Pretoria next week!"

"Oh my God, congrats, Proc! That's amazing. Now piss off, I'm sleeping."

The NYDA board induction comprises 10 full days of events and workshops, followed by dinners almost every evening with stakeholders with whom we need to establish working relationships. We are instructed on state protocol, policy, directorship of public agencies, the history of the NYDA, its role within the government, its goals, its key performance indicators, its duties, current projects, the fiscus, the organisational structure, the Acts of Parliament pertaining to our operations, the scope of our operations, the nationwide footprint and even diplomacy and international relations. It's a lot to get my head around.

Taking on this new responsibility is no walk in the park.

In early 2022, the NYDA has a huge task at hand: we have jurisdiction over about 10 million socio-economically disadvantaged young South Africans, a R1.19 billion budget and a team of 550 people in a country whose welfare feels more and more precarious by the day.

As a director, I am legally liable for the functioning of this organisation within my mandate of oversight and governance. This is a governmental agency within a government that doesn't have the most inspiring track record when it comes to delivering results. So, I know I have to go in 110%. I have a couple of mentoring meetings and calls with senior political advisors (including a man who helped a couple of the current African presidents win their respective elections) to train me up super-quickly on navigating it all.

It's a hell of a lot to handle. DigsConnect demands every inch of me, and I want to give it more than that. But I feel an undeniable duty to serve my country, to be part of the solution and not just wring my hands at the state of affairs. Look, when the president contacts you and tells you that you have been called up to serve, then you bloody well make a plan. You make it happen and get to work. No excuses, only output.

Often, I'll race off to a meeting in the back of an Uber with two meetings already running on different devices, along with a live phone call and someone sitting next to me trying to have a fourth meeting. It's insane. Having hardly recovered from major burnout, I probably should take a step back – but perversely enough, I find more energy by just diving back in.

Am I overcommitted? Almost certainly. But here's the

thing: if you can't ride two elephants at once, then what are you doing at the circus?

After ten full days of NYDA workshops and training, I return to the Digs team in Cape Town in mid-December, exhausted but exhilarated.

CHAPTER 30

BREATHING AGAIN

A new Covid-19 variant, Omicron, has just reared its ugly, spiky little head in South Africa. A team of South African researchers identified it. Although it is present across the globe, panic ripples across the world as people mistakenly believe that it originated here. As a result, many countries institute travel bans and shut their borders to South Africans. Things seem dire.

The country remains in lockdown. The feelings of powerlessness and uncertainty about the future are strong. We try to stay focused on our work, speccing new features and processing deals. Once again, I try to rally the team and focus everyone on the task at hand.

We keep going right up until 24 December, and then we close the offices for a desperately needed holiday break. The team members depart to the different parts of the country where their parents or families live. (Everyone on the team is between the ages of 21 and 26.) Then, on the morning of 28 December, hallelujah! It's the news that we've all been waiting for: the president has called an end to the lockdown.

The DigsConnect WhatsApp group immediately lights up. We're scattered around the country, so we jump on a group call, talking rapidly about the market opening up again and what we need to do to prepare. We agree to cut our holidays short and meet in Cape Town on 3 January to plan for what feels like a hopeful start to the new year. I'm in a rural village on the Mozambican border, where I've been spending my time in the ocean. I've also witnessed the most intense tropical storms I've ever seen, with lightning striking all around and palm trees being uprooted and falling over next to my tiny wooden bungalow. It's gorgeous and exhilarating. I've always loved violent storms.

I jump into my rental car and make my way to King Shaka International Airport to catch a flight to Cape Town. A day later, I'm standing in the boardroom of a co-working space with my team gathered around the table. This will be our new war room. With universities opening in just six weeks' time, we have to prepare for battle.

The country has been locked down for nearly two years. Some parts of the world are still in lockdown. Before Covid, we had a completely different business with a different model, different technology and a different team in a totally different world. Most of us haven't seen each other face to face in ages. We have no idea what to expect in terms of traffic on the site. While we have raised enough funding to get us to this season, it isn't enough to blow the lights out in terms of marketing. To be precise, our marketing budget is zero. I jump on the phone with one of our current investors, who agrees to loan us R100 000 for marketing expenses. That's it for our "blow the roof off" comeback season. We know we have to make it work.

After two years of lockdown, our valuation isn't exactly rivalling Apple's. In fact, with no transactions being processed through the platform, at one point during lockdown, our valuation for all intents and purposes hit zero.

The valuation is based on the gross merchandise value (GMV) methodology – essentially referring to the value of what is sold via ecommerce marketplace platforms. In our case, this is the value of the leases transacted through our platform. The more leases signed on the platform, the more valuable we become. Pretty straightforward. But if no leases are signed, which is what happened during lockdown, the company loses all its value.

And now, because we don't want to have a down round, we decide not to raise. If we hit our target for the season, we'll be on the right trajectory. We will have a positive cashflow and be self-sustaining – mecca for a founder – and raising will be a breeze. But if we don't hit our targets, we will once again face the end of our runway and an empty bank account. *Everything* hinges on this season.

CHAPTER 31

FREE TO WORK

It's 3 January 2022. I'm rocking back on my chair at my favourite coffee shop in Sea Point, waiting for Greg to arrive. I love leaning back on the rear two legs of the chair while resting the back of my head on the cool, green-tiled wall behind me.

As usual, I'm wearing a white high-waisted miniskirt and my on-brand white crop top. (The infamous "reckless" one mysteriously went missing one night after Greg came over for dinner. He openly hated that shirt but swears he's innocent. The jury's still out.) My shoes are off and my bare feet dangle above the floor. My hair is half up in a messy bun, and my sunglasses are perched in their usual spot on top of my head. Outside, the sun bakes down on the tar and the ocean is dazzling.

I've just gotten back from Mozambique. I'm 27 years old, my skin smells like the ocean and my hair smells like salt. It's high summer in Cape Town. All the stacking glass doors at the coffee shop are open to catch the breeze and the fans whirr above, moving the hot, dry air around the room. There's a smell of freedom in the air.

The coffee shop is popular with tech bros and VC bros, and every few minutes someone I know walks in, waves and comes over to say howzit. It's the first time in ages we're congregating again as a community, now that we've been let out of our lockdown cages.

Greg finally walks in, spots me and heads over. "One flat white, please," he tells the waiter.

"Another extra-hot latte, thanks, Mike!" I add.

"How was Mozam?" Greg asks. "Did you catch up with your mates from al-Shabaab?"

"Oh *ja*, of course. Compared notes on insurgency tactics and then passed the time playing poker and gossiping about our love lives during the tropical storm when the road was washed away. Cosy, you know."

"Nice, thought so." Now Greg gets serious. "So, the universities are opening. I've already started contacting our big landlords, and they're getting their properties up and running. We've got to move. Are you ready?"

"Are you?" I counter, grinning. "What have I always told you? I was born ready, stud muffin!" I try to wink, but it ends up looking like I'm having some sort of seizure.

"Jesus Christ, that was awful," says Greg. "Don't quit your day job, Proc."

We talk through the plan for the day. We'll soon convene a war room with our tiny band of ragamuffins that have held on through the storm. It's time to get to work.

That was the first Monday of the new year. As it was not long after the New Year's celebrations, people weren't yet thinking seriously about their plans for the year ahead, so there was no noticeable action on the Digs website. A few days later, by 7 January, we notice an uptick in our traffic – a small but discernible bump in our analytics. That's cute, we think. On the following Monday, 10 January, we have our usual morning standup where everyone runs through their goals for the day. Things on the site are still normal.

Then, around 11am, it's as if someone's flipped the chaos switch. Our traffic doubles, and then doubles again. This trend continues until to the end of the week as the booking enquiries start flowing in. Students are booking their accommodation so they can return to campus after two years of remote studying. The next week, the growth continues, doubling the previous record; a day later, it doubles again.

At this stage, the entire DigsConnect support and operations team consists of just two people, and there are already thousands of deals in the backlog. Our team is putting in 14-hour shifts, but we can't keep up. Greg and I end up processing 24 000 leads with our skeleton support staff. Landlords scramble to process the incoming leads after having retrenched their admin staff during lockdown.

On 29 January, our servers crash from the high volume of traffic. The entire dev team (two developers, a part-time product manager and a part-time UX designer) get on a call to try to figure it out. Our DevOps has been built by a back-end engineer who no longer works for us, and no one knows what on earth is going on. It's pandemonium.

All the while, thousands of requests are hitting our site and leading to a broken page. This is our make-or-break year, our BIG year, and we've done so well with our guerrilla marketing and getting our landlords ready – and now students can't even get onto the platform to make their bookings! I leap off my chair and run to the end of the road where I can scream in private. Are you bloody kidding me?! After I've slammed my fists against the outside wall like a child, I run back to the office.

The support lines start screeching off the hook. We keep getting pinged on social media, demanding that we solve the problem. Greg takes charge of the customer issues and pulls in friends and family to respond to calls and social media queries. I call in every favour I have ever been owed in Cape Town's tech ecosystem, and on a Saturday morning at 9am, we manage to get seven back-end and DevOps engineers – all from friends' companies – on a call to fix the issue.

No one knows what's going on, so we don't know how long it will take to sort out. I'd kill for a CTO to run the meeting, but we have none, so I have to figure it out. I ask one of the engineers to get to work on setting up a new server for us. This will take about two days, but at least I have a plan B if our current server fails and we can't restore it.

Technically, our DevOps is a super-complicated set-up, but because we've been underresourced and it hasn't collapsed yet, we've just kept sticky-taping it together and avoided resolving this technical debt – until it came back to bite us. But boy is it now biting us, like a huge black mamba that's gone for the jugular and isn't letting go.

The rest of the engineers start debugging together and, in an inspired moment that almost makes me fall to my knees with thankfulness, they figure out the issue and we're back up and running again.

Our analytics from that time still stuns me. The hockey-stick growth that in most cases is more parable than reality shows itself, and we ride this wave in all its glory, occasionally getting whacked in the face but learning to roll with it as we scale each new height.

By the end of February, we've hit our target. In one sense, we're lucky that the lockdown ended and students were so desperate to return to campus. But I'm also a big believer in increasing the surface area of serendipity. A strategic partnership goes a long way in stacking the odds in your favour. Again, it's funny how the dots connect. Nothing is ever really wasted when there's a real intention and a supreme effort is made. Our work hasn't escape the attention of the bursary providers: going into that year, we sign a partnership giving us the exclusive right to house hundreds of their students. On the other side of the equation, we have also become the official accommodation partner of almost every single private college in South Africa, and we have hundreds of landlords desperate to fill their beds after two years of vacancies. It's dry tinder, and we are the match.

So yeah, we make it. We make it. We go in swinging and come out on top. Against the iron-mail fist of two years of lockdown, through stress, amenorrhoea, terror and failure, we manage to hit our sales targets, increase our valuation and have an oversubscribed fundraising round, bringing in all the capital we need to secure our South

African business and launch our international business.

There is one little caveat. Our new international investors want us headquartered offshore, in or at least closer to bigger markets. At our board meeting, we reach a decision: DigsConnect will be headquartered in London. And I will be the one to move there.

CHAPTER 32

TOUGH TENDER

With Digs' global ambitions about to be unleashed, the outside world is calling, grabbing me by the arm and tugging at me to leave. Yet, South Africa is still holding me firmly by the other.

In early February 2022, I wake up in Cape Town on a Wednesday morning. It is 7.30am and the sun is baking. Naturally, the first thing I do is to swing my arm out wildly in search of my cellphone. I eventually locate it under a large pile of choc-chip cookie packets (all empty).

Straight away, my brain switches on. A message from an unknown sender on LinkedIn catches my attention. It mentions NSFAS. The National Student Financial Aid Scheme is a big deal in South Africa. It funds 690 000 of our 2.3 million students in higher education and training. I read the message: "Hey Alexandria, I'm sure you've seen the NSFAS tender that went out on Monday. Applications close on Wednesday next week. I think I'm the right kind of partner to make sure DigsConnect wins the tender."

I hardly raise an eyebrow at that. When it comes to government tenders anywhere in the world, there will always be characters trying to jump on the bandwagon. I duly disregard the message. What does surprise me, though, is the news of the tender, because it's the first I've heard of it. I quickly begin researching online and discover it is for the provision of an online student housing marketplace. The first part of the tender documents outlines almost exactly what DigsConnect already does: have a marketplace for landlords and tenants to connect. It fits us to a T. I can hardly believe that it spells out exactly what DigsConnect has done for the past four years. It's like they went through our platform and described it item by item.

The second part is about processing large quantities of cash between NSFAS and the landlords, which they call "accommodation partners". We haven't done that before. Handling that kind of money is daunting. It paints a massive red X on your back, and you become the mother of all targets for hackers, organised crime and even kidnappers in South Africa. But I can immediately see that this is an incredible opportunity.

I started DigsConnect to solve the student housing crisis. While we're making fantastic inroads, we are still David against the Goliath of entrenched superpowers in the sector. We are fighting the battle with our technology tools, with efficiency, lean opex and phenomenal customer service. Every time we get a message from a student who found their home on DigsConnect, our whole team reads it and grin at each other, knowing we're doing something great. Still, sometimes it feels like it's just a drop in the ocean that is the bigger housing crisis. I want to fix it.

And yeah, I am a founder who is obsessed with the stories of the Silicon Valley giants, pioneers who changed the way billions of people around the world experienced reality, who pushed our civilisation forward, who created the tools of modern life. I have a Steve Jobs quote for practically every occasion.

The NFSAS idea is appealing: to build the tech and systems that would support the housing needs of hundreds of thousands of people and go a long way in solving the student housing situation in South Africa. My head begins to buzz. If we get this tender, we can rely on our years of data and our relationships with our landlords who are telling us exactly what kind of solution they need from the government. The idea is terrifying and brilliant and wonderful. Hell, yeah! I want to do this.

I do some mental calculations. The number of students using the platform, if roughly half of the students were housed by universities, would be about 345 000. If the average national monthly rent was about R4 000 (NSFAS sets rental allowances based on the city, the courses being studied and other factors), it would mean R1.38 billion in rent transacting through the system every month.

I let that number sink in. "That's pretty hectic," I think.

I call Greg and get him up to speed on everything. When I tell him the back-of-the-envelope numbers, he is quiet for a second and then says, "That's pretty hectic."

"My boy, you took the words right out of my mouth. Obviously we're going to gun for it," I announce.

"Proc, have you ever done a tender before? It's no joke. It's a massive undertaking. Never mind even fulfilling the tender; even just submitting a bid. Have you looked through the bid documentation requirements yet?" he asks.

"I mean, kinda. But we'll get to the details later because this is *us*. Of course we'll figure it out! No problemo!"

"You mean, *you'll* agree to something and then I'll get dragged along and have to figure it out?" he replies, wearily.

"I love how we just know each other so well," I grin.

"Okay, let's meet up on Kloof and start diving into it."

I put down the phone, pop on my sunglasses and take off down the road.

I often feel like you need to talk stuff into existence. You can have an idea, but as you speak about it more and more, little paths for moving forward start popping up all over the show. If you don't speak about it, then those paths of opportunity will never appear. Some people might advise you to keep quiet when it comes to your goals, but I say, shout them out from the rooftops because the perfect collaborator might just be listening.

As it happens, later that same Wednesday, I have a drink with a friend, Timothy, who works in the broader Cape Town tech ecosystem. He is a venture capitalist who has followed the DigsConnect story with interest. I mention the tender and our apprehension about going for it, knowing that we are pipsqueaks in the face of something this size and the massive companies that will be competing against us.

"Hmm … I might know exactly the right person for you to speak to," Timothy says. "Have you heard of Evolve Technologies?"

"Yeah, of course!" Evolve Technologies is one of the

biggest government contractors for ICT in the country.

"One of the execs was at JPMorgan with me in London. I'll text him now quickly. When's the tender due?"

"Next Wednesday," I reply.

He raises his eyebrows. "Seriously? As in seven days?"

"Government," I reply, which is enough to answer his question.

I've always been comfortable with risk, mostly because during the 30 or so years of my existence, I've shown that I can usually carry it off. My mentor would often call me Jack Sparrow in disbelief as yet another one of my insane plans worked out perfectly. He would say, "None of this should have worked. How do you do it? Do you even know how you're doing it?" And, to be honest, I didn't. It was pure intuition guiding me.

I would spend time gathering data, observing, thinking and letting the pieces of evidence and premises swim in my mind. Then, suddenly – I don't even know how – my brain would align everything perfectly and, like a constellation, a pattern would emerge with beautiful clarity in a moment of insight that was almost transcendental. I'd then execute the idea with immediate effect. It worked, but it was haphazard. The path was never straight. It was a type of chaos theory.

The following day I call Timothy's contact at Evolve Technologies. I give him the pitch, and we realise that we have a better chance of winning if we work together. DigsConnect has already built most of what the tender requires and run it successfully for years, while Evolve Technologies has extensive experience in government tenders and processing large quantities of money.

On the Friday, we have a huge call with the Evolve Technologies team to figure out how the hell to put together a document of hundreds of pages in six days. We agree on what needs to be done – the commercial aspects, the technical details, the operations – and everyone gets to work. No one sleeps much that weekend.

Evolve Technologies is Joburg-based, but because of the tight timeline, their team offers to fly down to Cape Town that weekend so we can put the finishing touches to the document together. The bid must be hand-delivered to the NSFAS offices in Cape Town by 11am the following Wednesday.

Now, the wonderful thing about life is that it enjoys throwing a couple of curveballs at ya. That weekend, one of South Africa's main national airlines shuts down. A whole lot of flights are dropped, and passengers have to scramble for alternative flights. The lockdown has only just ended, so loads of people are flying around the country to reconnect with friends, family and colleagues they haven't seen in months, even years. For us, this means the Joburg team cannot get a single seat on a flight to Cape Town in time for the submission deadline.

No matter, I reassure everyone, Greg and I will figure it out. It's still high season for DigsConnect, so we are already pretty much at max cortisol dealing with that. By midnight on Tuesday, the eve of submission, we are still on video calls with the Joburg team to finesse the details. We call it a night at 2am and set our alarms for 5am to finish the submission, print the hundreds of pages, bind it and hand-deliver it by 11am.

I've been feeling a bit offish but have put it aside, thinking

I'm tired and that I will catch up on sleep after the bid submission. When I wake up on Wednesday morning, I feel as if I've been hit by a bus. I don't wanna say it's Covid, but I'd had it twice by then and it certainly doesn't feel dissimilar. But there is no time to be sick. I call Greg. "Look, I'm feeling like shit, might be Covid, hey. It might be best if I don't see you today in case I infect you?"

Greg doesn't miss a beat. "If you don't get your arse to my place now to finish this document with me, then you'll wish you just had Covid."

Right, fair enough. I stumble out of bed. Angela Merkel and I race along the M3 highway to get this monster of a document printed. I feel close to passing out, puking or both.

On arrival, Greg hands me a triple-shot espresso and looks ready to WWE-style body-slam me into focus. We have the Joburg team on speaker phone while they frantically bark out instructions on the documents to be reprinted after being reworked during the night. One of our interns has left to buy the binder and stationery we need to finish the document, but I tell her not to come inside in case I make her sick. I know Greg has too much willpower to get sick. Seriously, I could bring the black plague, TB, Ebola and the latest strain of Covid into the house and he will just be pissed off that I'm not working harder. I think he has too much disdain for incompetence to let himself get ill. He's genuinely a scientific anomaly.

We leave his house at 10.30am. It will take us 20 minutes to drive to the office where the bid has to be dropped off. We sprint towards Angela Merkel and try to decide who will be driving. Greg is possibly the worst driver on earth

– he once wrote off a car while going about 5km/h. To this day, not even the experts can explain how it happened. I'm a fantastic driver, if you consider the Dakar Rally to be the epitome of how to conduct yourself on urban roads, but I am doubled over by this point, dry-retching and seeing triple, so Greg has to man the wheel.

Defying death, we make our way to the NSFAS office while I try to put the finishing touches to the massive bid document. Greg hurtles the car to a stop outside the offices, mounting the pavement in the process and taking out the shrubbery, which is already looking feeble at the height of the scorching summer. We look around at the other cars in the parking lot. All of them are massive SUVs. Several have bullet-proof glass, and some of the people hanging around look like security personnel.

Sitting in my tiny Mini, we realise just how out of place we are. We're startup founders. We're scrappy, just kids. We operate by staying lean, creating grassroots value and winning customers by being great. This is government business; it's political, and not in a good way. These are the kind of people who make their millions selling to the government. It's the opposite of everything startups are about. This isn't about excellence; it's about box-ticking.

In South Africa, people are murdered over government tenders. It's serious money and serious business. There's often foul play. There are stories of people pulling out other people's tender documents from the bid submission box, so bidders usually stand around waiting for the tender documents to be collected.

Greg and I arrive at 10.55am. We tumble out of the car and make our way to the submission box. Everyone is eyeing everyone else. Bloody hell, it's like a Mexican standoff.

We jam our bid pack into the slot, giving it a punch or two to squeeze it through. We hear it thunk on top of the other documents. I turn around to see about 40 pairs of eyes watching me – huge men with hard faces leaning against their even huger SUVs, eyes hidden by sunglasses.

"Oh, hey, gents." I try to plaster on my usual saucy grin. I'm wearing the same shirt I slept in (a massive DigsConnect company T-shirt) and my hair is tied up in a messy bun on my head (and not in a cute Instagram-girly way). After days of not sleeping to get this done and being as sick as a dog, I look like I have just chewed my way through my straitjacket and escaped from the local psychiatric ward. The bags under my eyes can carry more water than 100 camels in the Gobi Desert. I am almost bent over with exhaustion. I get into Angela Merkel next to Greg and turn to look at him. "Just another Wednesday, hey?" We burst out laughing, which quickly degenerates into me having a coughing fit.

I'm home an hour later and sleep for a solid 12 hours. When I wake up the next day, I swear to God I have never felt healthier in my life. I've sweated out all the symptoms of the plague during the night, and I am pretty much ready to run a marathon and put the current Olympic record to the test. When I go down, it's fast and brutal. I spiral at close to the speed of light. But I rebound like one of those dreadful psychedelic bouncy balls that kids get when they win at playing arcade games. I hit rock bottom and then, before you can ever say, "You alrig–?", I'm already three miles up again. Cause here's the thing: I may sometimes be down, but I am never out.

CHAPTER 33

FULLY UNTENDER

We know that news on the NSFAS tender will take a while to arrive, so we throw ourselves back into our main work after the rush and chaos of the document submission. We feel confident about our chances. Yes, we're a young startup founded by two ex-SRC kids, but we think that amplifies our relevance since we have built a product for students, as students. Additionally, we are the only student housing marketplace in South Africa, with hands-on experience that gives us a head start. We have a huge proportion of the much-needed property stock already active on our database, strong landlord relationships, a great track record when it comes to service delivery and an excellent grasp of fair market value.

DigsConnect has not only pretty much all the large-scale PBSA (purpose-built student accommodation) providers on board but also thousands of beds coming from medium- and small-scale landlords across the country. These include landlords with two-bedroom apartments, four-bedroom houses or 20-bedroom buildings. These properties are too small and numerous for a state entity like NSFAS to consolidate and manage, but we have already vetted them and started processing their bookings. What's more, this smaller-scale, widely distributed property stock is crucial to get the kind of bed numbers needed to house all the students living off campus in South Africa – especially if the goal is to create a regulated system of safe, decent property options. So yes, we are confident.

A couple of months later, we get an email telling us that we are through to the next round and that we have to attend an in-person meeting to discuss our proposed solution. We are given 48 hours' notice. We're thrilled, but I have already moved to London. I desperately try to find a flight back home, but none will land in Cape Town in time for the meeting. Greg will have to go it alone. I feel like I'm letting him down massively by not being there. I am beyond frustrated with myself for being unable to get there on time.

Greg and I have a long call right before he is due to go in with the core team from Evolve Technologies. We run through the whole pitch again – all the possible questions, timelines and budgets. And then it's time for the meeting.

While they are in there, I nervously pace up and down a London street, intermittently checking my phone like a woman possessed, desperate for information. Finally, the phone rings. I answer on the first ring. Greg is on the other side, sounding calm. "It was good," he says. "I mean, I just spoke about the work we've been doing for years, so it wasn't like I was writing an exam and hadn't studied before or anything like that."

Now there is nothing to do but wait. And wait. And wait. We continue with DigsConnect, doing the exact same work that the tender called for.

We never hear from NSFAS again.

The news eventually breaks that the tender has been awarded to four other companies. Of course, I immediately look into all of them on the Companies and Intellectual Property Commission database and ask my network about their credentials. Only one of the four companies has a website, which does not work or contain a single property listing.

A couple of months later, the front page of the *Cape Times* newspaper reads: "Recordings cast fresh light on NSFAS scandal". The article says the CEO has taken "special leave" and that the board has appointed an advocate to investigate allegations made against him following the interviews during the tender process.

I remember the moment I read the headline. All the weeks of hard work and waiting for the tender flash through my mind. I think about the importance of NSFAS, and the key role it can play in breaking the poverty cycle in South Africa that is robbing our country of its future and people of their dignity. I think about the "virtual res" idea I pitched during the tender process: a distributed and decentralised residence management and accreditation system that would create jobs for thousands of students across the country, with network effects to increase the value delivered to students, landlords and universities year on year. I think about the tens of thousands of middle-class South Africans who have spare rooms in their homes, and how getting them on this system would not only mean good homes for students but also stimulate the economy at thousands of tiny touchpoints across the nation. I think about all the ideas we had, new ways to think about credit, about financial tools for young people, about using the power of technology to ensure that every student coming through NSFAS would experience the security of a place to call home. I think about all this intellectual property we would create for the benefit of South Africa, a global first. I also think about how we would finally show the world that South Africa is about more than load-shedding, race-baiting politics, a crumbling currency and violent-crime statistics. We would show that it's a country of resilience, innovation, collaboration, excellence and integrity. I think about how exciting it would be to use startup budgeting – lean and scrappy and bursting with efficiency – and apply this mindset and model to massive government budgets and deliver exceptional results in terms of bang for the taxpayer's buck. I think about the financial transparency we would create and the challenge of making something extraordinary for these students with all their dreams and struggles in front of them, who desperately need a place to call home.

And then I watch our chance to create something extraordinary disappear into the swamp of yet another NSFAS corruption scandal.

There are a million quotes I can throw at you here. Maybe one from Roosevelt; maybe a classic Churchill quip or a phrase from Steve Jobs. We all know the comeback lines. We all know that rejection is 99% of success. I won't bore you with any of these. Maybe I'll just share a text message I receive from my dad, who says: "Go for a long run, have a hot shower, eat a huge burger, go to sleep early. You'll be fine."

However, sometimes it just really fucking sucks when you lose. Sometimes you try to do something great, something good; you put time and money and effort and energy and life force and stuff you won't ever really get back into something – a project, a relationship, a company, a dream – and then you land squarely in the shit, and it just fucking sucks.

Maybe there's a lesson in that, and maybe there isn't. Maybe sometimes we don't need inspiration, the rousing speech or the magical sunrise after failure. Sometimes we just have to keep moving forward. Without inspiration. Without the feeling that you're working towards something. Without knowing what the hell it's all about. I don't know what drives us. I won't say it's discipline because I sure as hell am often in short supply of that. Maybe we just shouldn't overthink it. But I believe that the only real death is stagnation, and that the only way to leave a bad place is to take the next step out of it.

CHAPTER 34

PACKING UP

Before leaving for London in March 2022, months before we hear about our inglorious rejection from the NSFAS, the first step is to sort out my visa to work in the UK. I'm a South African citizen with deep, deep roots in this country and no claim to another nationality.

Luckily, the UK government has recently launched an "Exceptional Talent in Tech Entrepreneurship" visa to grow technology-related intellectual property in that country. As a founder with a few years of experience and something to show for it, I fit squarely into the mandate. I get the visa. My date of departure is at the end of March, right after my 29th birthday.

I ship my collection of books and art to my parents' house. In the weeks before I leave, my Camps Bay apartment looks like the ultimate ascetic's hangout. When I'm not rushing around, I sit cross-legged on the bare floor and eat poke bowls and ramen.

I also have to sell my beloved car, which is more

heart-wrenching than I'd like to admit. I'm dreadfully sentimental. I cry over all the spilt milk. Even unspilt, it'll get the waterworks going. But I have no time for sentiment. I work flat-out until a couple of hours before my flight is boarding. Between the NYDA, DigsConnect's busy season, the massive tender submission, my daily blogs, the YouTube channel I've started (and then abandoned and then restarted and then even more cruelly re-abandoned), it is all systems go.

It's our first post-Covid season, and we have to hit our sales target to close a round at an acceptable valuation. Thankfully, it turns out to be a brilliant season with students desperate to return to campus after two miserable years studying in their parents' kitchens.

We have an influx of bookings and overshoot our sales target. On track with our valuation goal, we are now gearing up for a raise, which is without a doubt the worst part of a founder's job. Give me 20 000 cold sales calls, give me eight months of technical debt to resolve, but please, God, don't tell me I need to raise. Every raise I have ever done has aged me by at least 25 years and reduced my will to live by about 78.9%. But it has to be done, so it's full steam ahead right up until the morning when I shove the last of my belongings into two largish bags.

I dropped one of the bags down a flight of stairs the night before, and it now has a monstrous, Great Rift valley-sized crack. Like any South African worth their salt, I have duct tape on hand to patch the old boy up. Unfortunately, my duct-taped bag makes me look like a drug mule, which is not a good look when you're travelling on a South African passport. Well, there is no time to get another bag, so I have to make it work and look as non-drug-muley as possible.

I drop the keys off with my landlord and take a last look around my Camps Bay apartment. I have loved this place so much. It's the first place I've felt at home. But there is no time to waste. My phone is going off like mad, and I need to get to the office and then to the airport in time for my flight.

As always, I have left everything to the very last second. I stay with the team as long as I can because that seems more productive than milling around some soulless airport lounge. When I finally glance at the time, I practically do a circus backflip out the window with horror. I hail a taxi as fast as these millennial thumbs can tap a screen and race to Cape Town International.

As fate would have it, about five billion tourists are bustling around between the check-in desks, with bags strewn all over the show and children stampeding like herds of buffalo in the Okavango Delta. The clock is ticking, so I sprint off, dodging between them like François Pienaar making his country proud. I skid to a halt at the desk, my duct-taped bag looking super-suspicious. The check-in man notes the urgency and, in the rush to check me in, catches my passport basically mid-air as I frisbee it at him. I chuck my bag on the belt and get mentally ready to Usain Bolt it to the security gate.

Once I am through, I head to the lounge to load up on snacks and send off a couple of emails. Unfortunately, I don't have much time to ponder the great mysteries of life because, as usual, I miss the announcements for my flight. Only when I hear them calling my name repeatedly on the intercom do I grab all my stuff and sprint down the windowless corridors towards my gate, leaving my iPad behind in the process. (Miraculously, I manage to track it down and have it shipped to me.)

As that last passenger who keeps everyone on board waiting, I do the walk of shame down the aisle to the back of the plane. I squeeze past the aisle-seat passenger into my window seat. It's time to take off and put my phone on airplane mode.

All the notifications, emails, calls and messages come to an abrupt halt. I look out the window at Cape Town, and it is all so quiet, so still. The fairground carousel of life shuts down, and the sudden change in momentum makes me feel a bit queasy. I'm soon comforted by the roar of the engine. Holy shit, this is happening. I am heading out into the world and won't be back in South Africa for who knows how long.

I had always felt like Real Life was somewhere *out there*, wherever the hell that was. Years of reading Sagan, Kerouac and Hunter S Thompson bred a mad desire in me to always keep moving, but during my gap-year travels I realised that I took my insecurities everywhere I went. Absolution wasn't to be found "out there".

As much as goodbyes suck, it's incredible how they create a sharp contrast in your life. Maybe it's something about the way the light falls as you're walking away.

CHAPTER 35

LONDON

I'm told that it's spring in London. As I walk out of Heathrow, a blast of icy rain hits me. "Fucking hell!" I do a 180 and run back inside to put on more layers of clothing.

Finding a place to stay in this sprawling city is a nightmare. It reminds me of my first year out of student res at UCT when I couldn't find a place to stay and the idea for a housing website like DigsConnect was seeded.

I feel achingly new in this massive place, this global city, London, the OG centre of the world, with my paltry rands in a city of pounds and the highest demand for space. I am so far on the back foot that I might as well be moonwalking. I start off renting short-term (and to this day I'm convinced that I'll never recover from that financially).

Finally, I manage to find a gorgeous shared flat in Chelsea with two British girls. It's on the outer edge of my budget, but I can just about manage it. I pay the deposit, and moving day draws closer. I'm so relieved to have found a place after more than 30 viewings and let-downs. One week before I'm supposed to move in, I notice that my deposit has been returned. "Odd," I think. I call the landlord. He doesn't answer. I send a text. "Heya! Noticed my deposit for the room has been returned, not sure if it was a mistake. All good?"

Three hours later, I get a reply. "Hi Alexandria, I'm gonna have to cancel your move in, one of the other applicants will be getting the room. The matter is closed."

My blood runs colds. I have by now given notice to my current landlord, and someone else has already taken the room. It would be impossible to find an affordable space in London at such short notice. I'm earning the UK minimum wage and quite literally do not have enough money to pay more for rent in London, and everything is already shockingly expensive. The 24 times exchange rate on my rands doesn't help.

It's almost impossible to open a bank account in London unless you have a permanent lease, and since it's almost impossible to get a permanent lease because of high demand, you're stuck paying with your foreign bank account and getting slammed with conversion fees all the time.

I try to call the landlord a few times. Eventually the number becomes engaged; he has blocked my number. Surely this is illegal? But what can I do? I'm a foreigner with no idea where to start or what to do, no contacts and nowhere to go. I text the other tenants. One of them replies and says that someone came to view the room and because it was a great flat in an amazing location, she offered the landlord more money than what he'd asked for. He said yes, and that was that. The irony of being the homeless CEO of a housing tech company does not escape me, but in the moment, I don't exactly find this to be a thigh-slapper.

Housing insecurity is an awful thing. Home is not just the place where you keep your stuff, where you sleep and cook and shower. It's your psychological state of security, of independence, of feeling rooted, like you have a stake in this world, that you're a part of it. It's the central point of our existence.

I end up moving into a friend's startup office on the South Bank. An influx of guys in their 20s occupy the apartment during the day to work on various startups. It's a hive of chaotic fun and constant activity, with the pack of always-hungry young guys eating, building, talking, creating and laughing all day. There are product launches, events and parties to attend, discussions, talks and an influx of remarkably accomplished and interesting people from every corner of the globe, all congregating in this eternal city while bursting with incredible knowledge and diverse ideas.

I often come home to find someone sitting at the kitchen counter, doing world-changing work, and I have the most insanely interesting conversations I've ever had in my life. My network explodes, my mind expands and the growth roof that I hit in South Africa is raised by a million miles. I realise how far a hungry founder can go in this world, and how small, in retrospect, my ambitions were back in Cape Town.

In London, I rub shoulders with founders, academics,

entrepreneurs, engineers, thought leaders, the occasional celebrity, actors, musicians, beauty queens, chefs, hoteliers and scientists who are all exploring the human experience and pushing the limits of what can be created – from VR, AI and crypto to the sort of articles that end up in *Nature* journal. Some of the people I meet have already sold companies worth billions.

We sit around on bean bags, eating sushi and talking about everything, or walk to Borough Market in a laughing mass of excitement as the future opens in front of us like a lotus flower. Their ideas and modus operandi blow my mind. It hits me: "Oh my God, I am living in *London!*" From tiny little Gqeberha, I've come to the most famous city on earth. And London has become my city. But I feel adrift and not really at home, because try as I might, I cannot find a place to live. There are rooms available, sure, but I can't find a place that I can both afford and be truly happy in. And so I can't bring myself to sign a 12-month lease for a broom cupboard and pay a small fortune to live there.

Being on an exceptional talent visa, I must meet certain salary and tax requirements in order to retain the visa. However, the dilemma of being a founder is that when you draw a salary, you're taking it from your company and that money in your personal bank account could have been used for marketing or hiring another mission-critical role. And so I have my salary capped at the UK minimum wage, which isn't helping my situation in one of the world's most expensive housing markets during a cost-of-living crisis.

The cool places that I find and love have people almost

physically fighting over them. You go to a viewing and 20 other people are there, a bidding war already on the go. Some people send me rejection texts when I don't get a room. Most just never reply. In a twisted way, it reminds me why DigsConnect's mission is so, so crucial.

Eventually, I know I have to move out of the startup office. I need another plan. An idea hits me one evening in June as I walk along the Thames to Tower Bridge. One of my best friends, another founder from Cape Town, has set up his secondary office in Berlin and is spending the summer there. He used to throw the most epic parties at his Bree Street apartment in Cape Town. I give him a ring.

"François! Cuz, do you have a couch for me? I'm coming to crash for a bit!" Because I've known him since our university days, we have the kind of friendship where no questions are asked if one of us invites ourselves over to the other's place.

"Yo, Proc! Haha, yeah, sure, pull in whenever. No couch but we have a beanbag on our office floor and it's all yours. We're in Mitte."

I almost sprint home to pack. London's housing situation has chewed me up and spit me out. When it comes to living spaces, I'm left thoroughly unimpressed with the city. If London is going to render me homeless, I will turn it into an adventure. Thankfully, I had the foresight to update my Schengen visa before leaving South Africa, so nothing stands in my way. I chuck what I have into a tiny bag. The next day, I land in Berlin.

CHAPTER 36

A GLOBAL HOUSING CRISIS

Amid a madly spontaneous series of events and random encounters with people across the beautiful continent of Europe, I set up shop in ultra-modern, edgy Berlin. There's a brilliant photo from that time, taken in François' Berlin office, of me sleeping on a beanbag in the corner with everything I own scattered in heaps on the floor.

A couple of weeks later, I make my way to Hamburg, and then on to Amsterdam. I live alongside a canal for a couple of weeks in a gorgeous suburb called the Jordaan. Along the way, I dive into the housing situation in the city, meeting local government officials, landlords and industry players. Amsterdam is experiencing a serious housing crisis as it fights for space from the ocean. In fact, in all the European cities I visit, I never once meet a single person who says, "Thank goodness there's enough housing!" It seems that this most fundamental need, the base of Maslow's hierarchy, is a global problem that still hasn't been solved and that the housing system is broken in almost every corner of the world.

I feel that the DigsConnect idea that evolved at the tip of Africa has global applications. There is clearly a worldwide need far more urgent than what I imagined. I also realise that I need an accelerant for our mission. I need a way to take our solution, improve on it and make it global. I become obsessed with making it the largest co-living and housing platform in the world.

I spend a while in the Jordaan, settling into a routine and encountering plenty of South African expats with whom I quickly bond. I also connect with a group of young German founders who invite me to work from their startup offices. I become a regular at a few coffee shops where the baristas know my order even before I speak. My Sundays are usually spent in Vondelpark where the tulips and roses are blooming one last time as autumn sets in. Sometimes we cycle into the countryside in this country of half-land, half-water. The Dutch are innovation-obsessed and incredibly future-focused, so there are always a ton of events on the go – relating to sustainability, future cities, architecture, modern agriculture and art.

Once the weather turns colder, I make my way to Lisbon, setting up shop in Cascais and then in Sintra. Portugal captivates me. Always being fond of a chat and forever striking up conversations with digital nomads in the cafés, I am invited to events and talks and meet extraordinary people with extraordinary stories.

I finally settle in a co-living space in Lisbon where I work and live for a while. One humid afternoon, I sit in my usual crossed-legged position on the outside couch on the huge veranda that overlooks the Portuguese Atlantic Ocean. My MacBook is perched on my lap.

It has been pouring with rain. The surrounding forest buzzes with birds and insects. My housemates have lit a fire inside, and the orange glow behind me feels incredibly cosy. I take a sip of my rooibos tea, which has gone cold.

My phone lights up as a text appears. It is a South African friend in London who knows someone who is moving out of her house and looking for a replacement tenant. The house is on a quiet road in Parsons Green, close to everything I need, including lots of green spaces. There is also the bonus of a massive South African community living in the area. I immediately call the outgoing tenant and offer to pay on the spot. Because the house is occupied by South Africans, two of whom know all about DigsConnect, they are super-keen to have me. Oh God, finally! While my European adventure has been incredible, for the past few months I've been homeless, rootless, without the peace and security of a place to call my own. It is time to make a home. Within minutes, I've booked a flight to London Gatwick the following day.

It doesn't escape me that I've only found a place to stay in London through a stroke of serendipity and not due to a built, scalable and viable solution. My resolve strengthens yet again to make DigsConnect the solution that everyone I met along the way will need. The global broken housing system is poised for disruption.

The following evening, I walk through the front door of the Parsons Green house. It feels homely. I arrange a mattress on the floor, with a lamp beside it. A pile of books and a few boxes serve as a desk. But before I have any real time to settle in, South Africa calls me back. My NYDA work has picked up, and DigsConnect's busy season is about to explode. I need to be on the ground for that. A fortnight later, I board my flight for Cape Town.

On the eve of my departure, it snows in London as temperatures plummets to a biting -4 degrees Celsius. I walk down to the small triangular park in the middle of Parsons Green and watch the perfectly formed flakes drifting around me. Behind the trees, a string of Christmas lights gleam magically. It has been a tough, lonely first year in London, but that night feels like the city's way of telling me to return.

CHAPTER 37

'FOCUS!'

I'm back in Cape Town and it's February 2023. It's summer again. I'm 29 years old, about to turn 30. It's almost five years to the day since we launched DigsConnect.

I'm sitting at our new office in Newlands. It's about 400m down the road from the Love Shack. The new spot is gorgeous, designed by one of South Africa's most brilliant interior designers. I'm standing on a balcony that looks out on Table Mountain, where a cloud is swirling through the forests just below the peak. The sun beats down. The African sky is wide and achingly blue. I breathe deeply. The air feels perfect, fresh, full; it almost feels *blue*, like I'm inhaling the sky itself.

I'm wearing a little white dress. It's got frilly straps and no back, cut low. Tremendously inappropriate for offices, I've been told. I think it's a huge improvement on my infamous "reckless" watermelon crop top. My huge, wide-brimmed white hat is on my desk. It's ostentatiously large and, for that, I love it. Next to me on a low coffee table is a copy of *Fast Company* magazine. My face is on the cover. Behind me, Greg is pacing around in one of the conference rooms, talking on the phone.

My call with Luke Nolan, the CEO of Student.com, is scheduled for noon. There are ten minutes to go. In my world, that's plenty of time for a coffee. Tight timelines are thrilling. I love to skate in at the very last minute. I can't help myself. It's my Jack Sparrow nature. It drives everyone demented because I'm told that I create far more stress than necessary, but there's just something so damn pleasurable about accomplishing things that should realistically be near impossible. My love of chaos and craziness, of just pulling it off, you know, rolling a six when the stakes are high, compels me. Tiny things like running to grab a latte before the meeting, just for the sheer pleasure of drinking it in this exact moment when I feel so electrified under the sun. I know it will make me happy. So, I dash off downstairs and skip across the road to the little hole-in-the-wall coffee shop. In a couple of weeks' time, at the end of February, I'm turning 30. The world feels like a ripe tomato. I can barely believe all that's happened over the past couple of weeks since I came home.

First there was the State of the Nation Address (SONA), delivered by President Cyril Ramaphosa, the same man who had appointed me to the board of directors of the NYDA. Well, actually, first there was the pre-SONA event at the British High Commission. It's always a superb experience, bumping into all types on the perfectly manicured green lawns and having fabulously heated conversations about South African politics across the political divide. I ended up standing next to André de Ruyter, the now ex-CEO of state power utility Eskom, just weeks before he would announce his resignation along with the subsequent publication of his explosive book, *Truth to Power: My Three Years inside Eskom*. We chatted animatedly about everything, from South African startups to the country's political future. The rest of the crowd was the usual collection of ambassadors, diplomats, politicians, business executives, NGO representatives and political activists.

The following night was the SONA address, which is a big deal in South Africa. When I walked into Parliament, I felt like Charlie clutching my golden ticket to enter Willy Wonka's magical chocolate factory. I had been to SONA before as an SRC member, but back then, I'd been shoved right to the back. Now I was slightly more than a yapping puppy among these big dogs. I sat next to none other than Advocate Dali Mpofu, one of South Africa's most well-known and controversial public figures and, at the time, the chairman of South Africa's radical far-left Economic Freedom Fighters (EFF). We struck up a conversation and were both howling with laughter within a couple of minutes, receiving furious glares from various "distinguished" guests.

As usual, SONA was chaotic. Dali was possibly in on it, perhaps orchestrating the disruption of the proceedings with EFF leader Julius Malema – including EFF members storming the stage before the event could start (standard practice for the party). Security rushed to the podium to protect the president, and a huge bun fight erupted as they tried to remove the EFF party members from the chamber. SONA was streamed live to the world. At one point, the camera panned over to where I was sitting. As soon as I noticed it was on me, I blew a big kiss to those watching at home. After the president's speech, I found some friends from different parties and we went to dinner to discuss this crazy, beautiful country of ours. All in all, an excellent evening.

Then I flew to Johannesburg, a city that I adore for its vibrancy and almost visceral crackling of ambition. I had a series of NYDA commitments around the province.

Organisational oversight and corporate governance are at the core of my role, but if truth be told, my heart is in being out there on the road, in the communities, being *in* South Africa and *with* South Africans in their homes and businesses, hearing their stories. Interacting with the human beings, not the numbers on spreadsheets and in budgets: that's the soul of the job. It makes the other part – sitting in dull, soulless, air-conditioned hotel boardrooms – bearable.

What strikes me most during this time is how far a surprisingly small amount of effort can go. Our agency might provide a piece of equipment to a tradesman or manufacturer that costs just a couple of thousand rand but which will transform their livelihood and life. I love this work.

On my second-last day in Johannesburg, I am eating lunch outside in the unbeatable Highveld weather when I am approached by one of the NYDA executives. He informs me that the person who is supposed to represent South Africa at the G20 Summit in India has been forced to cancel due to an emergency. My name has been put forward as a replacement!

Now, you know that I never say no to an opportunity.

"Focus!" countless well-meaning individuals have pleaded with me over the years. "Eat what's on your plate first!" they often add. But the thing is, I have a rather large appetite, so the whole idea that I'm "biting off more than I can chew" hasn't ever resonated with me. Doing a lot feels pretty normal to me, and like I always say, if you can't ride two elephants at once, then what are you doing at the circus?

Truth be told, it really is a manic time. February is always the busiest month of the year for DigsConnect. Students are starting university and the mad rush explodes onto our platform, jamming the phone lines as we sweep up most of our business in a few short weeks. Amid such an onslaught of traffic and attention, the usual chaos ensues and things invariably go wrong: platform malfunctions, increases in hack attempts, landlord–tenant disputes, developers patching bugs that pop up like whack-a-mole, people arriving at the wrong properties, last-minute leases to be signed, and team members on the verge of burnout as the phone calls stream in from students, parents, landlords, colleges and universities, all of them frantic, all of them urgent. It's madness.

CHAPTER 38

G20 & A GAME-CHANGING CALL

The invitation to attend the G20 Summit feels serendipitous. The opportunity has fallen into my lap. If I accept, I will be representing the NYDA and South Africa in the global arena, gleaning my first experience in geopolitics, international relations and economics.

I am desperate to understand the global commercial world and the gigantic power machine, to get to grips with what's feeding it and what's driving it. I want to get close to the heart of it so I can understand the motives, the logic and the soul of the beast, a huge, tangled web of international trade and transactions that all of us – every single person who has ever bought or sold anything on this planet – are a part of. Amid the countdown to my 30th birthday, the summit feels like an early gift and an opportunity that I cannot ignore. Without skipping a beat, I accept.

"Miss Procter," I am told, "the conference starts in three days. Your flight will leave Joburg tomorrow night."

Oh boy. It's go time.

I have brought almost nothing along for my meetings in Joburg, so I have to head back to Cape Town. I check online and discover a flight leaving for Cape Town within 90 minutes. As you've probably realised by now, I am horribly optimistic about my abilities and always assume I can pull things off that anyone with even a modicum of rationality and/or sanity would caution against. Whatever. There is no time for second-guessing.

"Buy the ticket, take the ride," Hunter told us, and I am all ears for that man. I wolf down the remnants of the lasagne on my plate and sprint to my hotel room to throw everything into my carry-on duffle bag. I then dash for the door.

On my way to the airport in an Uber, I look through the visa requirements for India. Because I will be travelling on state duty, I can use my official passport for members of government, which means I don't need a visa. Thank goodness. The green mamba (the South African passport) does not attract a red-carpet welcome from many other countries. We usually need a visa pretty much everywhere, and the wait times can be months. Even just the application process is laborious, almost always including in-person attendance at visa centres where delays of several hours are the norm.

Once I'm home, I realise that basically everything I own (which is, as always, in heaps on my bedroom floor) needs a wash. It's a really hot day. I can chuck it into the washing machine and have it dry by the morning. I load the machine, press "Start" and ... nothing. Are you kidding me? At this exact moment, the washing machine decides to pack up? Right, next option. I have recently befriended one of my neighbours in the building, an ancient lady with a crackling personality and a wicked sense of humour. I adore her. She always sits chain-smoking and day-drinking in the outside corridor and has me in stitches every time we speak.

"Rashida, darling, please can I use your washing machine? Mine's *vrekked* and I need clean clothes pronto!"

Rashida is a champ and gives me the green light. I then hop into my car and speeds off to the DigsConnect office to check in with the team and get stuck into work. En route, I buy two decent outfits at the Waterfront.

India is magnificent. It has one of the largest and fastest-growing economies in the world. It's the planet's biggest democracy and just became the first nation to land a rover on the south pole of the moon. It has a booming tech startup scene with more than 100 unicorns. But it is also ancient, with rituals and traditions that are an inextricable part of everyday life. It's a magical land.

When I land in Mumbai, it hits me just how fast life can change. The last time I travelled to India, I was 17 years old. I was less than a nobody, a scraggly, angry teenager fresh out of high school, staying in a dingy backpackers' for R20 a night. I was a failure by most standards of society. I had performed dismally academically at school, except for a few subjects. I had underperformed at sport, and I didn't have a lot of friends. I had been permanently on the brink of expulsion, and I had no offer waiting for me from a great university like Oxford or Stanford, unlike some of my peers. Back then, I was so angry. I constantly revolted against the "system". I was the outsider, the weird one, the loser.

As a teenager, I moved through the streets of Mumbai, Delhi, Jaipur, Agra and Rishikesh like a ghost, walking and taking buses while lugging my old backpack around. This time, I land in India and hand my government passport and G20 accreditation to the immigration officer. I'm taken to the VIP check-in and then ushered into a fancy SUV to be driven, with a police escort, to a 5-star hotel where some of the most powerful business leaders in the world are converging and where I will represent my country's youth and women. I look at myself in my corporate attire and G20 delegate accreditation and suddenly realise that *I am the system*. I am now a part of the decision-making bodies, the one with a voice and a seat at the table. What will my voice say?

I believe that if we want to change the system, we have to do it from the inside. We have to win by providing a better solution, by creating a better alternative, by building on our gains instead of breaking them out of frustration. We have to win by being better. In many ways, I am still that outcast kid. I always will be. And I love that my discomfort with the status quo lets me take a piercing look and, hopefully, see things for what they are. Building a fair system is hard. Creating genuine value with genuine craftsmanship is hard.

The G20 Summit is intense. Representing South Africa on a global political stage is an incredible experience: observing the fascinating dance between politicians and stakeholders, watching the interplay of macro- and micro-economics, and seeing how the networks of trade and the billions of transactions occurring all around the world culminate in industry and how policymakers scramble to erect guardrails and legislation around it all.

While there is much to criticise and improve upon in modern global structures, it is undeniable that we have come remarkably far as a species. I read Hans Rosling's *Factfulness* a couple of years earlier. With its undeniable optimism, it has become a huge influence on the way I view humanity.

At the end of the day, the only way forward is to keep improving on what we've learnt and to keep building despite the frustration we often feel when it comes to the breadth of continual human suffering and environmental degradation. Meaningful change on a massive scale is slow by nature. It's much slower to build than to break.

For a first bash at geopolitics, the G20 Summit was fascinating. It was 90% male and I was one of the youngest delegates by at least a decade. I'm firmly in the meritocracy camp and not a fan of quotas, but I did find it rather surprising that at a global forum of this size and calibre, more women and young people hadn't made the cut. The panel discussions particularly caught my attention as they were mainly "manels".

All in all, I listened, learnt and finally returned home with my eyes a little more open to the power structures of the world.

India will always be one of my great loves. I adore the country so much that just three weeks later, I returned to spend my 30th birthday in the Rajasthan desert with some friends I'd made in Jaipur.

After the summit, I return to Cape Town and get back into Digs work full steam. It is still peak season and pumping. We are doubling the number of bookings we made the previous year, and the mood is electric.

I've only been back for a couple of days when the meeting with Luke Nolan appears on my agenda – on the day I am wearing that white dress and the big hat and dashing from the Digs office to grab that 10-minutes-before-the-meeting cup of coffee.

Luke is always punctual. As soon as I log on to the call at noon, he is there.

"Proc! How you doing, legend?"

I crack a huge smile. Luke has an amazing energy that radiates good vibes.

"Howzit, Luke! So good to see you! Ja, jeez, things are hectic this side! Varsity is starting in a couple of days so the influx is in full swing."

We chat a bit about the business, going through some metrics, issues we're facing and various approaches to solutions. Luke has been doing this for years, so he can see the solutions in a second.

"I actually have some news for you," he says. "I'm going to be stepping down as the CEO of Student.com. The company needs new energy, and it's time for me to move on."

"Oh wow! That's a huge deal! How are ya feeling about it? What's going to happen next?" I ask.

"Well, the first thing is to find my replacement and start with a long handover. We've got some candidates lined up."

What he says next almost has me choking on my cappuccino.

"Proc, your name is also on the list. When you're in London, the investors would like to meet you and start the interviewing process."

Wait, what?!

Holy shit.

CHAPTER 39

THE DIGSCONNECT ACQUISITION

A few days after my Zoom call with Luke, I head back to London.

Luke and I had a pretty high-level chat about me potentially becoming CEO of Student.com, but it is a massive role and they will, of course, also interview way more experienced candidates. I might max out on passion, but the other candidates will certainly be classic business-leader types, more formally qualified and, well, more grown up. However, the decision-makers are clearly taking my candidacy seriously because I soon receive an invitation for a brunch meeting with David, one of the men who pretty much created the purpose-built student accommodation sector.

He is one of those extraordinary entrepreneurs who began creating businesses at a ridiculously young age and never stopped. He works with TDG, which has over time consolidated four companies, all to do with student housing, including Student.com. David is one of the players at the centre of a global network of housing, property management, tech and financing, so to be invited to what would become several meetings with him is a huge deal.

I don't sleep too well at the best of times, but I know there is little chance of getting any shut-eye the night before our meeting. Before I head off to meet David in Mayfair, Greg calls to talk me through the meeting.

"Okay, Proc, first impressions are crucial. You need to downplay the crazy. Speak slower, speak less, listen more and stay focused on what DigsConnect and student housing are actually about instead of talking about building human habitation on Mars, for God's sake. Alright? How are you feeling?"

"Exhausted, to be honest. Didn't sleep at all and my nerves are a bit on edge."

"What?! Exhausted? No time for that. I'm gonna need you to smash three espressos and stop whining. You know what we say, *eat a spoon of cement and harden up*. You can be tired later."

"Jesus, thanks for the sympathy!"

Greg doesn't skip a beat. "Okay, next, you can't go there dressed in your usual get-up of a 14-year-old who's just sneaked out to a party for the first time. What do you have to wear that's professional?"

This is a big ask. "Umm, how about the blue dress?"

Even though I can't see his face, it gives me great joy to imagine his pained look. "What the fuck! No! That one is basically more of a shirt than a dress!"

"Yeah, that's the best part!"

"Jesus Christ," Greg groans.

"Okay, okay, what about the plant suit? That's a classic crowd-pleaser. It's profesh, but still a bit spunky."

"Yes, perfect! That's the one! Don't forget to brush your hair, and don't be late! I'm going to call you every 10 minutes until you confirm you're there."

"We already share locations on Find My Friends."

"I'm calling anyway."

"Okay, okay. It'll be fine. It'll be fun!"

"I don't want fun. I want this to be a success."

"Great success!" I say in my best Borat accent, cracking up laughing. Greg just groans.

Despite my bravado, I am nervous. My old anxieties about my self-worth come roaring to the surface. I am often plagued by a desperate desire to prove myself, to be good enough, and in these moments of intense insecurity, I tend to overcompensate and come across like a total madwoman or, even worse, a sycophant. It's nauseating.

Try as I might to channel a soul-redefining revelation 10 minutes before the meeting and finally transcend into a tycoon of business, it doesn't look like this is happening. So, I will just have to make my way there as a flea of business instead. I spend a couple of seconds creating a hilarious skit about fleas in suits on Wall Street conducting business, and I laugh out loud. Focus, Procter! I have to get cracking! I still have to get to Mayfair from Fulham. With my nerves on high alert, the thought of getting on the tube during rush hour fills me with such dread that I decide credit card debt is preferable. So, I hail a taxi.

Quite possibly one of my favourite things in life is zipping through the streets of London in a classic black cab. Sitting in the back and taking phone calls, off to do Important Things in this Important City, makes this little flea of business seriously bustle with delight. Two minutes away from 5 Hertford Street, the location for our meeting, my phone lights up with a message from Greg. "You'll be fine. Just don't talk with your mouth full!"

The cab pulls up to the Mayfair pavement. I open the door in that fantastic way that makes it swing backwards. (Why do small things delight me so much?) I crouch down to step out and place one leather-clad foot firmly on the upmarket pavement. I look up and around, and my other foot steps out too. This is it. This is the moment. This is the start of Life 2.0; this is Alexandria Procter in all her raging glory, on her way to the top, unstoppable, ascending the corporate ladder, founder extraordinaire, maverick, icon, legend. As I take a bold step forward, my foot catches on the edge of the pavement and I go down like a ton of bricks right outside the front door, in full view of the concierge and the lah-dee-dah clientele coming out the door.

Well, fuck. I look like a real wanker now. I force a laugh that sounds more like the sound a car makes before its engine packs up completely. I hop to my feet, dusting myself off. Okay, I probably deserved that one.

The concierge is a master of tact and says nothing. After I check in for my meeting, I dash to the bathroom to make sure I don't look like a complete loony. (Mission failed.)

When I return, David and one of TDG board members who will be joining us for brunch are waiting for me in the foyer. We go through, sit down and start talking.

David is incredible – and not in the way I imagined. I had built him up to be this terrifying, aloof, movie-style tycoon. I immediately see just how wrong I was. He is real, grounded, funny, authentic and engaging. Yes, he is obviously intense, driven, ruthless when needed and ambitious to a level that inspires me to raise my own bar, but he is also very human. He is simply cool and an excellent listener. He is encouraging and kind but his gravitas makes it clear he has the authority. I like him immediately, and I know that I want to work with him. The more we chat, the more my conviction grows that, given the chance, we'd work really, really well together. In a sense, it feels like we're cut from the same cloth, two troublesome kids who stuck a middle finger to the status quo and built something ourselves. We click like Luke and I clicked.

It feels like DigsConnect could easily fit into the structure of TDG. While we eat brunch, we discuss what Greg and I built, the hard times, the good times, the lessons, the journey, and the balance of dreams and realism when it comes to building a business. I tell them all about the kooky ideas I had. I share my take on Student.com and where I believe it needs to go. I wax lyrical about the global state of student housing, the changing dynamics and the upwelling of massive competitors from the East. It is exciting. It is challenging.

As the morning progresses, I feel an interplay of nervousness, then a rapid flow of confidence and then sudden pangs of insecurity as we speak. I know I'm being observed the whole time, but more than anything, it just feels right. It feels like the massive space that exists when you leave an inland river and enter the ocean. Overwhelming, vast, disorientating and, finally, huge and free and roaring and wild and filled with billions of cubic metres of opportunities and chances in every direction you look. Eventually, I finish my dessert (a giant ice-cream-covered brownie) and we look at each other. It has been a good meeting. Eventually, we get up, small talk resumes, a couple of jokes are made and some hand-shaking takes place. They are staying behind for another meeting, so I say goodbye at the door where I fell so ingloriously a few hours earlier.

I walk out onto London's concrete pavements. It feels like I've just walked out of a dream. I head towards Hyde Park, walking faster and faster. Then I break into a run. I sprint through Mayfair's streets, down alleyways and across huge bustling roads, darting between red double-decker buses and shouting cyclists and leaping over whatever is in my path. I run with complete abandon. I'm not even thinking about anything, really; it's probably just the adrenaline, the weight of the future stretching its arms around me and flinging me forward. It feels tangible, like I can pluck it out of the very air I am breathing.

I am suddenly aware of all the choices that I made to get to this point, and all those I will make in the future – choices that will culminate in the story of my life. I can see the vision I am trying to create, a life that is worth living, the creation of something marvellous for humanity, my contribution to our evolving story of civilisation and the story of a human, a flash of life, in an otherwise cold and dark universe.

It feels like there is only one thing to do. I buy a humongous ice-cream and sit under a tree. I think of nothing else as I slowly lick it. Once I'm done, I wipe my sticky hands on my trousers and call Greg for a debrief.

CHAPTER 40

SHINE ON YOU CRAZY DIAMOND(S)

Over the following months, more meetings are held where I meet members of the executive team of Student.com and TDG. I am even sent for a leadership assessment by one of the top business coaches and facilitators in London (who also works with British MPs). Upwards and onwards we march.

During this time, Greg and I fly to Chamonix in south-eastern France in the Alps for an invitation-only student housing conference and skiing trip alongside British and European leaders in student housing and property. It is a fantastic experience (and my first time skiing – a sport with which I fall in love almost immediately).

When the time comes for DigsConnect to expand beyond South Africa, we choose the UK as our global headquarters because we believe the cultural overlap with South Africa will be easy to manage. While the synergy is clear, the degree of maturity of the markets is worlds apart. During the conference, we get to see this. The more we listen and engage, the more we realise just how little we know, how big our ambitions for a global footprint are and how much we're on the back foot. But we are among whip-smart, hilarious and highly successful individuals who are more than willing to welcome us into the fold. The entire experience is a privilege that we do not take for granted.

With so much happening, it feels like everything is falling into place around the Student.com and DigsConnect merger. In my mind, stepping into the role of CEO is making more and more sense. I've done a deep dive into all my original founding documents for DigsConnect from the early days – and I mean *early,* before the company was even a company, before there was anything solid or anyone else steering the ship.

I've looked at the ridiculous, brightly coloured pieces of cardboard that I used for my study notes and then as DigsConnect's dream boards. They took me back to a time when the constraints of reality and experience did not exist, when, with a child's sense of wonder, I'd pictured what "home" could come to mean to anyone who didn't really known what home was or who simply needed to make themselves a new one, to feel safe, to have fun and to belong in a place to be proud of.

Now I start extending this vision beyond DigsConnect, turning it into a seed that I want to plant at the heart of Student.com. This is an incredible opportunity, an unbelievable moonshot, and while I respect what exists and all that has been done, I know that I have to go in there and make it my own. I need to craft it with my life experiences, my soul and my love for this ecosystem.

Finally, after months of discussions, assessments, conferences and conversations, we agree in principle at my final meeting with the Student.com executive team that the deal will go ahead. It makes sense. It feels right. Greg and I start gathering information to form a more coherent mental image of what we are taking on. (One of the non-negotiables from our side is that Greg and I are a team and, if they want me, he will be part of the package too.)

I begin writing documents to prepare for my "first 100 days in office" so that there will be no guesswork, only focus and productivity. In a series of three intense meetings in three days, and after consulting our key investors, we draw up the term sheet. And then ... nothing.

We wait. And wait. We try to follow up. Then we wait some more and follow up again. There had been some conflict around whether we would do a share exchange, an outright buyout or a structured buyout with a partial exchange, but it hadn't seemed like an insurmountable obstacle, just something that needed a clever solution to suit all parties – like any deal. We also know that the executive team is pursuing much larger deals in the US. Still there is no word.

In the background, we still have the partnership agreement we signed with Student.com two years previously in Dubai, and we have a phenomenal relationship with their team, many of whom I consider friends and with whom I've spent loads of time at dinners and theatre shows, in pubs and on the slopes of Chamonix. But now I start to see that the current partnership allows them pretty much full access to the inner workings of DigsConnect, and I realise that the acquisition isn't a matter of two friends shaking hands with everyone's best intentions at heart. This is business. This is a negotiation between two parties on opposite sides of the table, with different and even competitive interests. It dawns on me that we are weakening our position by hanging on limply and waiting for them to throw us a bone. It puts us on the back foot. It verges on pathetic. It is not the sort of behaviour one would want from an incoming CEO who is expected to steer a company into global domination.

So, I call Greg. "We need to end the partnership with Student.com. You know I love those guys, but with no indication on whether the deal is going ahead or not, we're holding DigsConnect in limbo. We're holding off on other investments, we're holding off on growing in this market, we're putting our lives, our company, our investors and clients in limbo and sitting around on our hands.

"This isn't us, Greg. We're not the kind of people to let other people decide our fate. We've always done it ourselves. We have to. We always have. It's always been you and me, on our own, figuring this shit out and building it from the ground up. The hard way has always been, and will always be, the right way. We need to get back to work."

Greg is silent for a moment. Then he speaks. "We were so close to bringing these two companies together and creating something epic here. You know I've spent the last couple of weeks reorganising their org chart, thinking through the budget, optimising on spend, getting to grips with the different markets where we'd be operational … But Proc, I agree with you."

"Look, never say never," I say. "It isn't a no. It's just

that it's faded into the background for them. We need to stay relevant, and the only way we can do that is by being great. Being a great company must always be top of mind. Invention is not disruptive. Only customer adoption is. We keep increasing traction and keep making our company too big to sideline. Not for anyone else, but for ourselves."

"Once we cut the partnership, we lose all the global stock. That's over one million beds. We'd lose our whole PR pitch as Africa's largest student housing marketplace," Greg says.

"I know, and that's a shit one to lose. But let's be honest, it was always a vanity metric. It was completely out of our wheelhouse to try to do all of those locations. If anything, spreading our focus like that was probably one of the biggest hindrances to our actual progress," I reply.

Greg sighs deeply. "Righto, back at it, Procco?"

"Always, Greggo."

A few weeks later, we go on to raise a small funding round and then add two revenue verticals, including a property management arm we call Weego – a play on TDG's property management company Yugo (a bit of cheeky banter that's right up our alley). We cut costs and double down on our dogged determination for increased profitability on our own terms.

A couple of months later, Greg and Dylan move to London, where, after more than a year of mostly working in different cities on two continents, Greg and I are finally working alongside each other again every day on our new global vision for DigsConnect. We split our time evenly between Cape Town and London, doubling our bookings in South Africa year on year but with a firm foot in the global arena.

One morning, we meet at Battersea Power Station just after sunrise to sign the contract for our new global headquarters' office space. It's an iconic location. As we stand outside the building, the moment feels big. Some things just click, you know. I've often seen the power station while I'm walking around London, and on the cover of my dad's LP of Pink Floyd's *Animals*. He and I listened to it on countless Sunday mornings while eating fried eggs on toast, when I was a little girl back in Port Elizabeth, when I told him, "Just wait, Dad, one day I'm gonna change the world. You'll see."

FINAL THOUGHTS

The motto of Y Combinator, arguably the world's most famous startup accelerator, is: "Build stuff that people want." That statement is a tad more abridged than an MBA thesis, but nuances aside, everything does come down to this.

In the startup world, it's called "value genesis". During those early days of DigsConnect, it was a great lesson to learn first-hand, especially in South Africa. I also realised that my job as a founder was to generate revenue for the startup, and profit thereafter, as fast as possible.

Money gets a bad rap, particularly among my fellow millennials and Gen-Zs. And if you're like me just a couple of years ago, you'll think this view of revenue generation above all else is myopic and that you know better. You might believe that your unique vision of an insanely cool product that you've come up with will magically lead to a massively successful company that will save the world and end poverty, but then you're likely to get lost in the details of how you'll keep the lights on at the end of your runway.

These days, Greg and I always remind each other that

a good business is a boring business, because boring businesses make money. A successful company creates profit for its shareholders. That, in turn, drives your valuation, which is quite literally the value of your company and an indicator of how good you are at value genesis. The word "shareholder" comes with baggage and images of greedy billionaires. But it's so much more than that. A shareholder is a human being who backs your vision, hears your story, looks at your numbers and decides to give you their hard-earned money so that you can create more value for them and for society as a whole. They give it to you with their trust. In exchange, your job is to make sure that you give back x10.

This is where I start to get philosophical. Once I began to understand economics – not from the perspective of a disgruntled undergrad quasi-communist sitting in a lecture theatre at UCT while still being bankrolled by someone else yet thinking I was entitled to an opinion on the economy – my perspective began to change. I now see the world through the eyes of an active, tax-paying citizen whose very life and freedoms are tangled up in the crazy web of our global economy. Once I began to understand that I was a player in this game along with eight billion other people and that life was sometimes inherently unfair, I began to see just how goddamn beautiful and extraordinary it all was. There's a rush of excitement knowing that we can build anything, spurred by the boldness of our creativity.

And then, looking beyond our planet, our mote of dust in the greater cosmos (would I be a tech entrepreneur if I wasn't a Sagan devotee?), this extraordinary flicker of civilisation and consciousness is the only one we know (so far). Protecting and furthering this fragile light is everything. To choose to create, to commit ourselves every day to placing one brick on top of the other, all in pursuit of a kinder, smarter, more sustainable and more inclusive world – I believe that is the real revolution.

ACKNOWLEDGMENTS

When I think of Melinda Ferguson, my publisher and very hands-on editor, she stands tall, grinning, winking and loving – an utter colossus. We met just under two years ago when I asked for writing advice on my blog. I told her my story, the DigsConnect story, and straightaway she saw that it could be *Upstart*, this crazy little book that you're holding.

Mel gets me in a way that few do. She knows when she needs to crack the whip, and then she threatens my very life and safety to get me back on track with focus and deadlines. She knows when to create a space of kindness, safety, warmth and quietness for me. She knows when I'm taking things far too seriously, and she'll crack me up with her brilliant humour.

Writing comes naturally and easily to me, but it flows fast and chaotic, like turning on a tap that turns into a firehose. When I started sending Mel millions of different documents with disjointed storylines, tens of thousands of words with spelling errors and repetitions or whole chunks missing, she wove her magic and pulled it together, editing and shaping the chaos into something spectacular – into this very story. She's gone over and above as a publisher and as an editor. My girl, I bet you didn't think that when we signed this contract, I'd be calling you at all hours, sometimes in a tornado of energy and sometimes in tears, and somehow, perfectly, you've always guided me back to shore. Thank you for everything. This book would not exist without you.

I also need to talk about Thalia Bruinders. Tals once told me that in our lives we get seven soulmates (or something like that; you know I'm not the best at listening). I know that you are one of mine, and I am one of yours. Born five days apart in February 1993 and ending up as roommates at DSG at 14 years old, we became best friends. I knew I'd love you forever. More than 15 years later, that's been true every single day, even though there have been times when life took us down different paths. Knowing that you're alive out there somewhere in the world gives me so much joy. You dreamer, you poet, you lover: your soul is one of the purest ones out there.

Gregory Ramsay-Keal. I'm not going to say much about you here because this whole damn book is basically about you, ha ha. But what I will say is that being a founder is more than a full-time job. It demands every inch of us. Over the past few months, my duties at the NYDA and working on this book have taken up time that I normally would have put into DigsConnect. You supported me in a way that I will never forget, stepping up to lift the load so that I could complete these projects. It's difficult for me to say in a few short sentences how much you mean to me, which is probably why I wrote a book about it. Thank you. I've got your back – always.

Dad. My safe harbour. I tell you all the time how grateful I am for everything you do, but I should probably tell you every day. Thank you.

Mom. The funniest and most brilliant person I know. We haven't always had the easiest relationship, but calm seas never made a skilled sailor. You were the first upstart.

Kate and Stuart. Completely mad, completely loving; you guys are champs. Can't wait for another Gqebby Kersfees on the stoep by the pool. Thanks for keeping me humble.

A big shoutout to our investors, who heard our story and gave us the rocket fuel to take this thing to the moon. Thank you for backing us, for fighting with us and for laughing with us. What a journey!

It takes an ecosystem to raise a startup. The Cape Town tech startup ecosystem of founders, teams, structures and events all celebrate and champion the magic we're creating at the southernmost tip of Africa. The stories of your work inspire more people than you can imagine.

To every single aspiring founder who has ever DMed me on social media to tell me about their dreams or to tell me how the story of Digs made them believe they could also build something: I read every single one of your messages again and again, and they mean the world to me. Keep building.

I also need to thank all the DigsConnect users, customers and partners; every landlord, every student, every university and college; every partner, every single person and every institution that at some point created an account on our platform or signed a partnership deal with us. Every single person who found a home on our platform, every landlord who found a tenant for their property, and the tens of thousands of users who have connected on our platform. Every interaction, every conversation, every booking, every new listing, every review and every story from people who have told us what the platform means to them – you're the reason we're doing this. It starts and ends with you. Thank you.

And finally, my first and deepest inspiration: South Africa. Dawn rises in Mzansi like the massive yawn of a lion. I often say our country is a miracle, and every day I see the proof. I could not be prouder and luckier to have been born into the budding democracy of a young country at the tip of an ancient continent, a country that is finding its feet and fortifying its soul with a mantra of "stronger together". You are a country of a million laughs and a million heartbreaks, proof that the very best of humanity can and will triumph. A shining light to inspire a world of peace.

I have enduring gratitude for living in a world and society where it's possible to take a moonshot. For a life with all its limitless possibilities, all its hope, all its beautiful fragility and all its fleeting wonder. Every second is a blessing. Every struggle is a gift. Whatever it is that made all of this possible, thank you.